The Adobe PageMill™ Handbook

The Adobe® PageMill™ Handbook

Hayden
Books

Paul Kent

Gary Stein

The Adobe® PageMill™ Handbook

Library of Congress Catalog Number: 95-62408
ISBN: 1-56830-272-X

Printed in the United States of America 1 2 3 4 5 6 7 8 9 0

Warning and Disclaimer

Publisher	Lyn Blake
Marketing Manager	Ray Robinson
Acquisitions Manager	Karen Whitehouse
Publishing Manager	Laurie Petrycki
Senior Editor	Lisa Wilson
Acquisitions Editor	Karen Whitehouse
Development Editors	Brian Gill, Laurie Petrycki
Copy/Production Editor	Bront Davis
Technical Editors	Brian Gill, Laurie Petrycki
Publishing Coordinator	Rosemary Lewis
Cover Designer	Aren Howell
Book Designer	Gary Adair
Production Team Supervisor	Laurie Casey
Production Team	Heather Butler, Tricia Flodder, David Garratt, Aleata Howard, Erika Millen, Beth Rago, Erich Richter
Indexer	David Savka

About the Authors

Paul Kent is president of Mactivity, Inc., the computer consulting company he founded in 1984. Today, Mactivity is a worldwide leader in providing Macintosh information via its conferences and publications. When Paul isn't thinking, talking, or writing about the Mac, the Internet, or networks, he likes to play basketball and golf, attend San Jose Sharks games, and hang out with his daughters Stephanie, 8, Jillian, 4, and Emma, 3. Paul and his family live in Los Gatos, California—the coolest town in northern California—where he and his wife, Terrie, love to exercise, try out new restaurants, and play with their dog Bagel the beagle.

Gary Stein is the Web Czar for Mactivity, Inc. He has a master's degree in Literature from Chico State University. An avid mountain biker and reader, Gary helped create the Mactivity/Web conference and serves as its master of ceremonies. He also teaches a Mactivity seminar called "Publishing on the World Wide Web with your Macintosh" around the country. He lives in Santa Clara, California, but his appeal is universal.

Trademark Acknowledgments

All terms mentioned in this book that are known to be trademarks or service marks have been appropriately capitalized. Hayden Books cannot attest to the accuracy of this information. Use of a term in this book should not be regarded as affecting the validity of any trademark or service mark. PageMill is a trademark of Adobe Systems, Inc.

Dedication

From Paul:

This book is dedicated to my wife, Terrie. I can't imagine a greater source of inspiration than her support of whatever I do and the way she makes raising our three daughters look easy. She makes me laugh, think, and learn. No one should have it this good....

From Gary:

To Karen, thanks for the understanding of the long hours. And, of course, to Mom and Dad without whom this would not have been possible.

Acknowledgments

The authors want to acknowledge the following people for their contributions to this book.

The staff at Mactivity, Inc. who make the discovery of new ways to use the Macintosh, networks, and the Web fun, challenging, and interesting.

Our friends at Hayden Books: Karen Whitehouse, Laurie Petrycki, Brian Gill, Bront Davis, and Lisa Wilson, who helped us to make this the best book possible.

The creators of PageMill: Bill Kraus, John Peterson, Robert Seidl, and Roger Spreen, for their vision to bring Web publishing to the masses.

Hayden Books

The staff of Hayden Books is committed to bringing you the best computer books. What our readers think of Hayden is important to our ability to serve our customers. If you have any comments, no matter how great or how small, we'd appreciate your taking the time to send us a note.

You can reach Hayden Books at the following:

Hayden Books
201 West 103rd Street
Indianapolis, IN 46290
(800) 428-5331 voice
(800) 448-3804 fax

Email addresses:

America Online: Hayden Bks
Internet: hayden@hayden.com

Visit our Web site at: http://www.mcp.com/hayden

Contents at a Glance

Contents

Foreword

We're pleased and excited to bring some of the cutting-edge topics that we've presented in our Mactivity/Web conferences and seminars to a wider audience. As with our conferences, our goal is to educate, entertain, and enlighten you. We hope you will find the practical application of the software presented in an enjoyable, digestible format. We've garnered quite a reputation with our conference attendees for knowing what to teach and how to teach it. This book provides a great opportunity to bring our approach to the widest possible audience and complement the fun we have in our face-to-face events.

The World Wide Web is a fascinating phenomenon. Everyday a newscast, television commercial, print ad, or business card is directing people to "check out our site" on the World Wide Web. The societal change is interesting because it is so pervasive. The wealth and variety of information is astounding. It seems that everyone from David Letterman to your favorite sports team has a home page on the Web. Having a Web site, however, is more than the latest, trendy electronics gadget. The World Wide Web is altering the landscape of communications in our world on a daily basis.

Within this social shift, another change is occurring. Web publishing is evolving from the hands of Webmasters to the hands of people who simply want to convey information. More and more, Web "surfers" are trading in their surfboards for the tools that enable them to publish information that is important to them. *The Adobe PageMill HandBook: Web Publishing without HTML* is significant because PageMill is the first tool that puts Web publishing technology into virtually everyone's hands.

People always have had a lot to say, but they never have been able to say it to an audience the size of the Internet. As we see it, there are three reasons why the Web is so appealing:

■ **Cost.** With desktop publishing applications such as PageMaker, you can create a document containing your theories of the universe, but the cost of printing and distributing your publication would be high. Personal opinions, the results of research, artistic works, poems, comic strips, photographs, audio or video information (bandwidth permitting!), almost any type of personal expression can be posted, relatively inexpensively, on a Web page.

The tools required to publish on the Web are readily at your disposal. You probably already have a computer and a modem, or you certainly have access to one. At $99, PageMill is a bargain! The only other costs are Internet access and a fee to serve your Web page from someone else's machine. Many Internet service providers offer members space on their Web server. The average annual expense of a dial-up Internet account, however, is still much less than printing and mailing a 4-color brochure to 1,000 people. In addition, you can change the material on your Web page whenever you want, you can use as many colors as you want, and you have an audience of millions.

■ **Availability.** The Web is like the gift that keeps on giving. In one sense, the medium is static—it's always there. Yet, it's constantly changing. No matter where you are, you can tell people to check out your Web site and point them to a static location. In today's overhyped, overmarketed world of junk mail, junk faxes, and telemarketing calls, information where you want it and when you want it fits the way we work and communicate.

■ **Fun and Easy.** Human beings get a kick out of communicating, technology, and themselves. The Web is a synthesis of these three things. Creating information that is meaningful to you is an expression of yourself. Putting that information in a place where other people can get it is like putting a little bit of yourself out there. You're inviting feedback, commentary, and criticism. In other words, you're inviting communication. When someone takes the time to email you with comments, questions, or suggestions for your Web page, it feels great! Your information has actually affected someone enough to take action. If you do it really well, you'll find that a community will start to build around your online publishing efforts. After all, the people who check out your Web page have something in common regardless of race, color, creed, age, or nationality. They are all interested in what's on YOUR page. When you get over the God Complex you experience from having your information affect people in this way, you'll come down to earth and recognize how really cool electronic communications are! Add to all this the fact that you command all of this incredibly cool technology (even though you're not entirely sure how it all works), and you've satisfied some really basic needs as a plasma unit in the 1990s.

Let's set one caveat here. In the same way that Adobe PageMaker brought desktop publishing to the masses, it also is responsible for an avalanche of ugly, poorly designed documents that have invaded many of our daily work environments. Mismatched headlines, 20 typefaces on the same page, and a wealth of other typographical and layout faux-pas provide coffee-room fodder for graphics artists around the world. Even great software can't make you an artist. We'll teach you how to use the tool and direct you to some valuable resources, but the rest is up to you.

Web publishing is still publishing. Although new design paradigms are being discovered all the time, guidelines that successful, traditional media publishers follow, such as knowing your target audience and designing accordingly, absolutely apply. Whether you are publishing a Web-based newsletter for your colleagues at the elementary school, or putting your community's Little League schedule on the Web, designing a site that is appealing, informative, timely, and useful to your readers is a common sense lesson to apply to your project. Why do it if no one is going to read it?

We wish you the best of luck in your journeys toward becoming the next William Randolph Hearst, Malcolm Forbes, or Simon and Schuster on the World Wide Web. It's incredibly rewarding to put a piece of information out there and know that people all over the world can and will look at it.

Drop us a line and let us know what you think of this book. Better yet, join us at one of our Mactivity/Web conferences and tell us in person.

Why surf when you can make waves?

Paul Kent   President of Mactivity

> paul@mactivity.com
> http://www.mactivity.com

Gary Stein   Web Czar

> gary@mactivity.com
> http://www.mactivity.com

Introduction

Welcome to the exciting world of publishing on the Web
with Adobe®PageMill™. With this program you don't need to
learn the cumbersome HypertText Markup Language
(HTML) to get your information Web-ready. PageMill
provides a WYSIWYG (What-You-See-Is-What-You-Get)
interface that enables you to focus on the content and style
of your Web page instead of learning a computer language.
PageMill provides a simple, integrated environment for
editing and previewing your HTML documents in one
program.

Objectives of This Book

This book teaches you how to create pages that can be published on the World Wide Web. You will learn text formatting, the use of lists, use of graphics, how to create clickable imagemaps, and the creation of forms. Each chapter teaches you practical skills to create visually interesting pages. The chapters build upon each other so that, by the end of the book, you will have both a mastery of the PageMill program as well as an understanding of Web publishing techniques.

The term *Web publishing* is the process of putting information into a Web-presentable form. A Webpublisher can be anyone who has something to say or has information that he or she wants to make available. Businesspeople with product catalogs, for example, might want to use the Web to publish their material.

A *Webmaster*, on the other hand, is someone with a wider range of Web skills. A Webmaster is responsible for managing and configuring the Web server. He usually addresses networking issues associated with a Web server and creates or employs special applications that extend its functionality.

Most Webmasters are Webpublishers, however, not all Webpublishers are Webmasters. *The PageMill Handbook* focuses on Web publishing without requiring any knowledge of networking, server management, or computer programming. Without PageMill, publishing information on the Web requires HTML knowledge. With PageMill, Webpublishers can create Web documents and transfer them to Webmasters for inclusion on Web servers. In addition, experienced HTML coders can use PageMill to generate Web pages faster and easier than traditional methods.

 Note

Before creating Web pages with PageMill, you need a working knowledge of the Macintosh. You should understand how to use the mouse, be familiar with Macintosh menus, windows, and standard commands such as opening, saving, and closing files.

More experienced Webpublishers can use PageMill to reduce development time. Because the application provides an integrated environment for previewing and editing, you'll spend less time creating pages. *The PageMill Handbook* will show you how to use PageMill to create all the basic components of a Web page and then how to integrate advanced, browser-specific HTML tags using PageMill's Raw HTML command (see Chapter 7 for more information).

 Note

> The difference between Webpublishers and Webmasters will probably diminish in the future as interest in and access to the Internet continues. Someday, people will reach for a Web publishing program, such as PageMill, as often as they do a word processing program. Wouldn't it be great if your Macintosh operating system came with the capability to serve Web pages in the same way Apple FileSharing enables your Mac to be a file server today? Imagine professors posting their office hours, Little League coaches posting the teams' practice schedule, and shop owners posting business hours and sales items on the Web right from their desktops. When PageMill was demonstrated to us for the first time, Robert Seidl, the president of Cenenca Communications, (the company that originally wrote PageMill) described his vision of the Web as being the "dialtone of the future," meaning that soon people will reach for information on the Web as naturally as they reach for the telephone today. If the wide and diverse use of the Web today is any indication, the Web will probably be the primary conduit of personal and business information before the next century.

Publishing Without HTML

HTML describes a set of markup commands that tell a Web browser how to display the various text and object elements of a Web page. HTML uses a syntax where you turn on and off effects by using predefined codes called tags. Here's a simple HTML example:

```
<H1>Welcome to the EmmaZone</H1>
```

The text Welcome to the EmmaZone is enclosed by the tags <H1> and </H1>. The first tag, <H1>, tells the browser that all the text that follows is to be formatted as a first-level heading (you'll understand what a first-level heading is later) until the browser encounters the end tag, </H1>.

The benefit of HTML is that it formats text and images in a standardized manner for browsers running on all computer platforms. The procedure goes something like this: browsers know how to read HTML, PageMill knows how to generate HTML (it just hides the complexities by providing you with an intuitive interface); ergo, when browsers read the pages you generate with PageMill, they are reading HTML.

The corollary here is that you are bound by the same constraints and issues as someone constructing his Web page by writing HTML. So, even though you'll be publishing without using HTML, there are a few things about HTML and browsers that you need to know:

■ Some HTML is displayed differently on different browsers

You don't have any control over this. These inconsistencies are a part of the Web. Even though HTML is a standard, various browser manufacturers implement the standards differently. Though these usually are subtle differences, they are differences nonetheless, and a good Webpublisher will have several browsers available to test what the output will look like.

■ Netscape Extensions

Netscape Communications is one of the main commercial organizations fueling the Web. They are the creators of the immensely popular Netscape Navigator browser. Because Netscape Navigator is used by so many people (an estimated 80 percent of the market uses Netscape Navigator), Netscape finds itself in the enviable position of being able to introduce

FYI

The Web community debates whether it's better to create pages that utilize Netscape extensions or to design pages for the HTML 2.0 standard. Many Web pages state: "This page looks best when viewed with Netscape 1.1," and often provide a link for the netsurfer to download that browser. Some people in the Web community want to define a set of standards so that one company can't dictate de-facto standards. Some say that waiting for standards slows innovation, and the market should decide whether their extensions should be accepted as the standard. Ultimately, the market will decide, although the debate continues.

its own extensions to HTML without waiting for the standards organization's approval. Pagemill implements some of the Netscape extensions but not all.

■ Control

It's important to understand the control you have in designing your Web page, and what control you give up depending on the user's browser.

A user can set his browser's preferences to determine what fonts are used, the size of the text, and the colors used for fonts, hypertext links and backgrounds. You cannot override these controls, and you need to be aware of these issues to make design decisions.

The PageMill Handbook will help you to understand what you do and don't have control over when designing your pages with PageMill, and the choices you need to make about designing for various browsers.

Fortunately, you won't have to learn the cryptic HTML, because PageMill generates the commands for you. You can, however, view the standard HTML codes by opening your pages' data files in a text editor.

Do you still need HTML? Eventually, you might want to learn some HTML so that you can do some of the more advanced tricks or take advantage of browser-specific features. Without a doubt, PageMill gives you a rich set of tools that enables you to get your information Web-able in the simplest manner possible. If your goal is to publish information on the Web, PageMill is all you'll ever need.

What You Can Do with PageMill

Here's a simple explanation of what you can do with PageMill:

■ PageMill is a graphical tool for creating Web pages on a Macintosh. These pages can be served via an HTTP (HyperText Transfer Protocol) server, also called a Web server, to other people connected to the Web.

■ PageMill provides a single environment for creating pages, viewing the pages, and testing hypertext links to other pages.

■ PageMill provides a functionality for creating clickable imagemaps, which otherwise require a special program. Imagemaps enable you to define *hot spots* on images that, when clicked, take users to other other pages.

■ PageMill's support of the Macintosh drag-and-drop architecture makes it easy to create libraries of commonly used Web-page elements.

Beyond the Scope of PageMill

Following are some features that you will not find in the current version of PageMill. You will, however, find some of these items in future versions of the program:

■ **An Internet browser.** You cannot surf the Web with PageMill. PageMill's Preview mode enables you to test hypertext links and to view documents stored on your computer the way a browser will display them.

■ **A CGI authoring environment.** CGIs (Common Gateway Interfaces) are applications that run in conjunction with Web servers and extend their functionality in some way. Some CGIs, for example, enable Web servers to pass information to and from a database, and others keep track of how many times a page has been accessed. PageMill currently does not provide an environment to create CGIs.

■ **Support for Netscape extensions.** In the ever changing world of Web standards, PageMill currently does not support Netscape's implementation of tables.

■ **A Web server.** PageMill can't serve pages over the Internet for people to view. To do this, you need special HTTP server software such as MacHTTP (a shareware program), WebStar by StarNine Technologies, NetAlly by Delphic Software, or InterServer by InterCon Systems.

■ **A site management tool.** Managing a Web site means maintaining the links between local and distributed documents. The sister product to PageMill, Adobe® SiteMill™, provides this functionality.

Additionally, the HTML standard that imposes many limitations on Web publishing, restricts PageMill as well. The range of typographic and page layout control available in a desktop publishing program like Adobe® PageMaker®, for example, is simply not supported by HTML or, consequently, PageMill.

Using This Book

The PageMill Handbook provides information for Webpublishers of all skill levels. To help you use the book more effectively, we provide the following special features.

 Tips and Notes

Each chapter takes you from beginning, introductory concepts through advanced techniques. Tips and notes provide helpful information to Webpublishers of all skill levels.

FYI

Occasionally, we've added additional background information that might be of interest to you.

Throughout the book we provide easy-to-reference Command Summaries. These summaries provide steps to using PageMill's many features and tools. An example of a Command Summary follows:

Aligning Text

1   Type the following text into your new PageMill document:

Greetings from Asbury Park, N.J.

The Wild, The Innocent and the E Street Shuffle

Born to Run

Darkness on the Edge of Town

2   Highlight the text and select the Center Align Text button from the tool bar.

Talking to the Webmaster

As you design and create Web pages with PageMill, you'll undoubtedly have some questions for the people managing the server on which your pages are posted. These sidebars will help you communicate with your Webmaster.

 A CD icon indicates a file that can be found on *The PageMill Handbook* CD-ROM.

Getting Started

If you don't have a retail version of PageMill, this book's CD provides a demo version for you to acquaint yourself. (See the last page of the book for installation instructions.)

If you haven't already done so, install your demo copy of PageMill from the CD in the back of the book. Don't worry if you don't know what to do or what you want to publish, that's what this book is for.

Chapter 1

Introduction to PageMill

This chapter provides an overview of PageMill. It identifies the various features of the program and how to use them. You can get your feet wet with a few simple exercises as you build your first Web page using PageMill.

A Tour of PageMill

The PageMill interface looks like a Web browser. It has two modes: Edit and Preview.

You can use Edit mode to build a Web page or a collection of pages, called a *Web site*. Text layout and formatting, the placement of images and objects, and the creation of hypertext links are functions found within Edit mode. When you open a new page in PageMill, you are in Edit mode.

Preview mode enables you to see what your page will look like on a standard Web browser and to test the hypertext links you create to other pages that reside on your Web site. Although PageMill has the appearance of a Web browser, it is not a functioning Internet browser; it is a Preview browser. You cannot "surf" the net using PageMill, nor can you use it to read newsgroups, send electronic mail, create markers to other Web sites, or perform any of the other tasks associated with Web browsers. PageMill is a Web page layout program. It is designed to look like a browser so that you, the Web-page author, can preview how your pages will appear on a fully functional browser.

 Note

When you open an existing Web page in PageMill, the program opens the page in Preview mode. When you open a new Web page, the program opens in Edit mode.

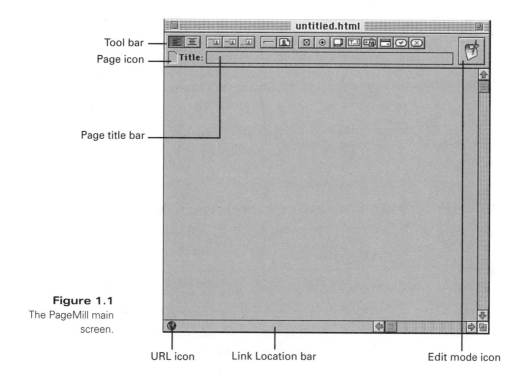

Tool bar

Page icon

Page title bar

untitled.html

Title:

URL icon   Link Location bar   Edit mode icon

Figure 1.1
The PageMill main
screen.

The PageMill Window

The PageMill window has the following three main areas:

- Tool bar

- Content Area

- Link Location bar

Double-click the PageMill icon in the PageMill demo folder. (If you haven't installed the demo application, see the instructions on the last page of the book.) Choose New Page from the File menu to create a new window. Now you're ready to follow along.

You are presented with a New Page window when you launch PageMill. Most of your Web-page creation takes place using these three areas. We'll look at PageMill's other windows a little later in this chapter.

The Tool Bar

The tool bar is part of PageMill's main window (see Figure 1.2). Each new page that you create with PageMill has its own tool bar. Even if you are working on several documents, each document has its own tool bar. The tool bar contains a collection of buttons that enable you to do the following:

- Insert images and horizontal rules on your Web page

- Align text and images on your Web page

- Enter your Web-page window title, which will appear when someone loads your Web page

- Create forms

- Access the Page icon for creating links

- Move between Edit and Preview modes

For more information refer to Appendix B.

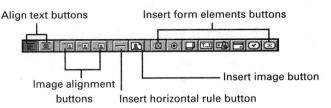

Figure 1.2
PageMill's tool bar.

Align text buttons · Insert form elements buttons · Image alignment buttons · Insert horizontal rule button · Insert image button

When the cursor is placed over a button on the tool bar, a description of the button's function, if it is available to you, appears to the right of the tool bar. A large icon, conveniently located in the upper right corner of the PageMill window, enables you to switch between PageMill's Edit and Preview modes. The graphic on the icon changes depending on the mode. You'll also find the Page icon, the heart of PageMill's powerful drag-and-drop capabilities for creating hypertext links, at the far left of the tool bar. You can create hypertext links in PageMill by dragging the Page icon to a place on the page that you want to link. (This can be accomplished only with the full version of PageMill.)

Note

Documents need to be saved for a link to be created.

The Content Area

The Content Area is where you place the text, graphics, form fields, and other elements that make up your Web page (see Figure 1.3). Like the text area of a word processor or page layout program, the Content Area is where you layout and manipulate the pieces of your Web page. To enter text, click in the Content Area to create an insertion point and begin typing. Alignment and formatting commands can be applied from menu commands or with the Attributes Inspector (see Chapter 3). Page elements, such as horizontal rules, images, and form elements, can be added by using the tool bar. In addition, you can drag-and-drop text and graphics to the Content Area.

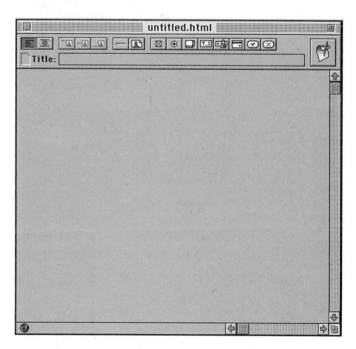

Figure 1.3
The Content Area.

The Link Location Bar

URL
. . . .
URL stands
for Uniform
Resource
Locator.

The Link Location bar, located at the bottom of the PageMill window, is where you enter URL addresses for hypertext links to other Web pages both on your Web site and on the Internet (see Figure 1.4). It is a standardized way of assigning an address on the Internet. (See Chapter 2 for a detailed sidebar that explains how to use URLs.) In Preview mode, URL addresses dynamically appear in the Link Location bar as your mouse pointer passes over the text and graphics that have hypertext links associated with them. In Edit mode, you need to select the entire linked text or graphic to view and edit the link.

Figure 1.4
The Link Location
bar.

Link Location bar

PageMill's Other Controls

In addition to the functions available in the main PageMill window, you will use three other controls to produce your pages. The Attributes Inspector and image view are discussed in greater detail in Chapters 3 and 4. Here's a preview of them, and PageMill's other window, the Pasteboard.

The Attributes Inspector

The Attributes
Inspector is
invoked by
selecting Show
Attributes
Inspector from
the Window
menu or by
pressing ⌘-;.

To follow along, activate the Attributes Inspector by choosing Show Atrributes Inspector from the Window menu or pressing ⌘-; (see Figure 1.5). The Attributes Inspector is PageMill's command center. It functions as a floating palette that you can position anywhere on the screen. Unlike the tool bar that is located at the top of every PageMill document, there is only one Attributes Inspector. If you are working on several pages at once and have the Attributes Inspector open, it acts on the page that you currently have open. The Attributes Inspector is used to view and set attributes relative to page appearance, such as text styles and various objects that you have placed on your Web page. You can move among the three modes of the Attributes Inspector by clicking the icons in the upper-left corner of the window.

Figure 1.5
PageMill's
Attributes
Inspector.

Page Attributes

Page Attributes mode enables you to configure background color, foreground color, and link color (see Figure 1.6). This also is where you apply those cool background patterns that have become so popular. Finally, you can specify a CGI (Common Gateway Interface) script location. CGI scripts can be used to extend the functionality of a Web site. See Chapter 5 for more information about CGIs.

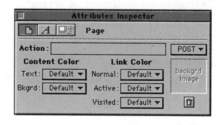

Figure 1.6
Attribute Inspector
in Page Attributes
mode.

Text Attributes

You can use the Text Attributes mode of the Attributes Inspector to turn selected text into hypertext links and control the appearance of the text (see Figure 1.7). Most of the controls available under style attributes also are found as menu options with Command key (⌘) equivalents (see Appendix A). Their availability as checkboxes and pull-down menus in the Attributes Inspector provides a handy alternative to menu options for controlling text.

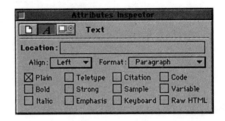

Figure 1.7
Attributes Inspector
in Text Attributes
mode.

Object Attributes

Object Attributes provides control over selected forms and image objects. The options available in this mode are different depending on whether you are setting attributes for form elements or images. With PageMill, you can create input forms to collect information from readers of your page. When creating forms, Object Attributes enables you to name your form elements, assign their default values, and in the case of text fields and text areas, specify the exact size they should have. When using the Object Attributes mode of the Attributes Inspector (see Figure 1.8) to control images, you can do the following:

▐ Scale and size graphics

▐ Define borders

▐ Identify the image as a static picture, a clickable imagemap that links to other Web pages, or an image used as a Submit button

Note

See Chapter 2, "Working with PageMill," for more information about forms.

Figure 1.8
Attributes Inspector
in Object Attributes
mode for images.

Tip

For advanced HTMLers, we've included Appendix B, which maps the Text Attributes to their HTML.

The Pasteboard

The Pasteboard (see Figure 1.9) is activated by selecting Show Pasteboard from the Window menu (⌘-/). It's like a Clipboard where multiple text and graphics elements can be stored. Logos, copyright notices, and icon bars are examples of elements that you might want to keep on your Pasteboard. The Pasteboard provides you with five pages for easy organization of frequently used items. Each page can include multiple items, and the Pasteboard can be sized using the size box in the lower right corner. Like many parts of PageMill, the Pasteboard supports Macintosh drag-and-drop technology to simplify the transfer of text and images. When you place text that contains hypertext links into the Pasteboard and later drop that text into another page, the links are maintained automatically.

Figure 1.9
The Pasteboard.

The Image View

The image view provides a powerful integrated facility for working with graphics. It enables you to use your graphics as clickable imagemaps that have hypertext links connected to different parts of the graphic. It also enables you make an image's background transparent so that it blends in with the page. Finally, you can specify if an image is to appear saved as an interlaced GIF. The correct height and width attributes for the image are automatically specified, which enables the browser to display the page much faster. Open the EarthAndWare Tutorial folder in the PageMill demo folder created when you installed the demo. Drag-and-drop the file flowerPots.gif into the Content Area. To activate the image view, double-click an image (see Figure 1.10).

Interlaced GIFs

Interlaced GIFs come into focus gradually as they are downloaded from the Web server to a Web browser.

 Note

For more information about using graphics and interlaced GIFs see Chapter 4, "Imagemaps and the Image View."

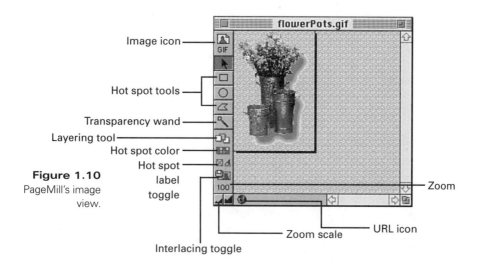

Image icon

Hot spot tools

Transparency wand

Layering tool

Hot spot color

Hot spot
label
toggle

Figure 1.10
PageMill's image
view.

Zoom

Zoom scale

URL icon

Interlacing toggle

Creating a Page

Now that you know where everything is located, let's get familiar
with PageMill in a more hands-on manner. Launch PageMill by
double-clicking the PageMill icon. If this is the first time you've
launched the program, refer to the last page of the book for
installation information. Close any open windows in PageMill and
Create a new page by selecting New Page from the File menu.
Remember, this is a demo version of PageMill, so you cannot save
your documents.

Creating a Page

1 Single-click in the Content Area to create insertion point.

2 Type: **Welcome to my first Web Page!**

3 Highlight the text that you typed.

4 Apply a style from the options in the Style menu by choosing
Emphasis.

continues

5 Turn off the style by reselecting emphasis in the Style menu.

6 Apply the Bold style from the Style menu.

7 Click the center text alignment buttons in the top left of the tool bar. (PageMill only supports center and left text alignment.) Single-click to the right of the exclamation point to deselect the text.

8 Press Return twice.

9 Type: **Welcome to My World**.

10 Highlight the text.

11 Choose Heading from the Format menu.

12 Hold down the mouse button and select Largest from the hierarchical menu under Heading.

13 Release the mouse button.

14 Click at the end of the text string.

15 Press Return twice.

16 Select Paragraph from the Format menu to turn off the Largest Heading setting.

17 Click on the left text alignment button.

18 Now enter more text. Type the following:

You've reached the home page of <Your Name>. Welcome! I'm just learning how to create Web pages using this great, new program called PageMill. If I had known it was this easy, I would have started long ago. This page is all about me. I hope you like it. Here's a picture of me.

19 Press Return twice.

20 Now click the Insert Image button in the tool bar.

21 In the File dialog box, select milkhead.gif from the Images folder within the EarthAndWare Tutorial folder.

22 Choose Open in the File dialog box.

23 Next, click the Horizontal Rule button in the tool bar. Insert a horizontal rule.

24 Move the cursor to the Title field of the tool bar.

25 Click to place the insertion point.

26   Type: **The <Your Name> Home Page**.

27   Press Return.

28   The title you just entered will be seen as the Window title when someone views your home page with an Internet browser.

29   Now view your document in Preview mode.

30   Click the Mode Toggle button in the upper right hand corner.

31   Return to Edit mode by clicking on the icon again.

Summary

Congratulations! You have just completed a quick tour of PageMill and created your first page. This chapter discussed the main PageMill window, the Attributes Inspector, the Pasteboard, and the image view. In addition, you created a basic Web page that included headings, a graphic, a horizontal rule, and body text.

You've now navigated through most of the basic functions you need to create a Web page. You're ready to dive into PageMill's advanced features and build even cooler Web pages. Although there's much more for you to know, it won't get much harder than this.

Chapter 2

Working with PageMill

PageMill has a number of tools that enable you to create impressive Web pages. This chapter takes you step-by-step through using some of PageMill's most popular tools—the tools that you'll use most when creating Web pages.

How to design a Web page is entirely up to you—there are no hard and fast rules for Web-page design. This chapter is designed to help spark creative endeavors. It begins with the basics: manipulating and placing images; and then moves on to a somewhat advanced topic: creating forms.

Basic Web Design

There are as many different Web-page design philosophies as there are Webpublishers, so create your Web pages in a form that feels right for your anticipated browsers. Do not assume that what you see in PageMill is the same as what you will see in a Web browser. Each browser may interpret HTML differently, and each reader can set his or her browser to read documents differently. Items such as fonts, colors, and graphics will likely look different on a browser than they will in your PageMill document.

Given this uncertainty, each project you design should be evaluated based on its content and goals, not on how it looks to the eye. How you divide your pages is a primary consideration. Should your page be one long page, or should you break your content into several pages? This depends partially on the amount of content that you want to present and how users interactively move from one block of content to the next.

The Home Page

In general, Web sites are broken into sections and pages. Sections are often divided by headings (text set in larger type than the rest of the content), rules (horizontal lines), or graphics. A Web project generally begins with a home page that describes the information contained at the Web site. The home page typically is accompanied by a number of support pages that include more specific information (usually the home page's subtopics).

A home page might introduce the reader to your site, give some information about what is offered at the site, or tell who created the site and why. Of course, all this information depends on the type of site you are creating.

Home pages can have a clickable imagemap that has pictures, icons, or images that represent navigation clues for the Web site (see Figure 2.1). A simpler way to display this is to offer a table of contents that links viewers to specific places on the Web site.

Figure 2.1
A home page that enables you to navigate through the Web site via a clickable imagemap.

Support Pages

Support pages, on the other hand, might include a common graphic as a header to give the site consistency and identity, yet might contain more textual information (see Figure 2.2).

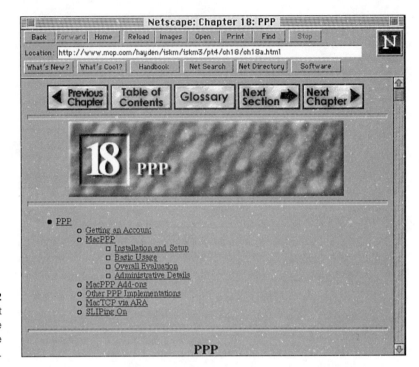

Figure 2.2
A support page that you navigate via the scroll bars or a table of contents.

The Audience

Another factor you need to consider when creating Web pages is the audience. After all, you're publishing information for the public. Understanding certain characteristics of your audience helps you make smart decisions when designing your page.

Some of the more important issues include deciding what browser capabilities your audience will have, and what type of Internet connection it has (modem, ISDN, T-1, and so on). This will help you decide what information you serve, how you serve it, and how big or how many graphics and images you place on your page.

Setting Preferences and Getting Organized

Before you begin creating Web pages, configure PageMill's preferences to specify where your files are going to be stored.

Organize your Web projects with a master folder, and then create subfolders within this master folder for individual projects. At the root level of the master folder, create a folder to hold all images. Begin by choosing your Images folder or creating a new folder as described here:

1 If not already open, launch PageMill by double-clicking on the application icon. If already open, save and close existing pages. If you are using the PageMill demo, the save function is disabled.

2 Select Preferences from the Edit menu. The Preferences dialog box appears.

3 From the Image Preferences section, click the Default Folder for Images folder (see Figure 2.3). Another dialog box appears.

4 Use the standard Macintosh navigation methods to identify the folder you want to use as the default folder for holding images. Click the In Here button (see Figure 2.4).

5 Click OK in the PageMill Preferences dialog box. Do not quit PageMill; you will use it when you learn how to format text.

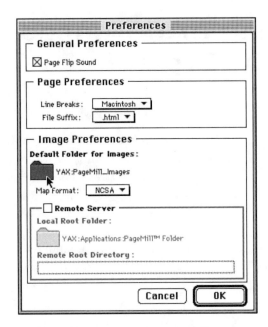

Figure 2.3
Click here to
choose the Default
Folder for Images
folder.

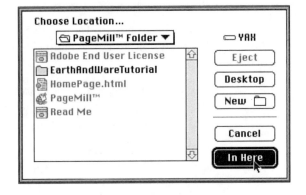

Figure 2.4
Choose a folder in
which you would
like to store your
images.

Now you're ready to begin working with PageMill. The rest of the chapter will concentrate on the tools you'll need to create your own Web pages.

Page Formatting

Open a new PageMill document by choosing New Page from the File menu (or by pressing ⌘-N).

When starting a new page, give your document a title; do this by entering text into your document's Title field. For this example, type **I'm a Web Publisher** (see Figure 2.5). This title will appear in the title bar of a Web browser's window when someone loads your page.

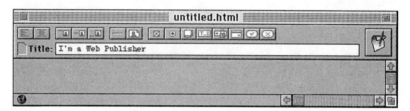

Figure 2.5
Entering text into the document's Title field.

Save your page by choosing Save (⌘-S) from the File menu. Once saved, you'll notice that the Page icon (at the left of the tool bar) becomes available (see Figure 2.6). The Page icon will be used for creating drag-and-drop hypertext links.

Figure 2.6
The Page icon becomes active after you save your document.

Tip

When you save your document, PageMill will add a suffix of .html to your filename. It's a good idea to keep this suffix, because it is proper HTML style. Alternatively, if your Web pages will be served or viewed by a DOS-based server or browser, you will need to do two things. First, keep your filename to eight characters or less. Second, use .htm as a suffix rather than .html. DOS can only read filenames that are in the 8.3 format—eight characters with a three character suffix. For example, homepage.htm would be a legal filename, while homepages.html would not (nine characters and a four character suffix).

You can have PageMill save your files with an .htm suffix by selecting Preferences from the Edit menu and choosing .htm from the file suffixes popup menu. Alternatively, you can make the change each time you save the file.

Headings, Styles, and Rules

The simplest tools for organizing a Web page are headings, styles, and horizontal rules. Headings represent different sizes of text that are used to create titles for sections of your Web page. Horizontal rules are useful for visually dividing sections of your Web page.

Headings

Headings come in six sizes. The headings look like those shown in Figure 2.7.

The sizes Large through Largest typically are used for headings. To turn text into a heading, highlight the text and choose the heading size you want by selecting Heading from the Format menu.

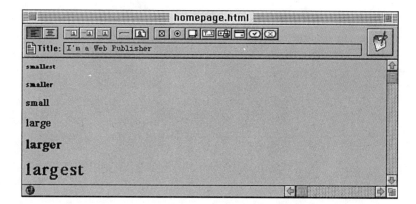

Figure 2.7
PageMill offers six
heading sizes.

Styles

Two types of styles are available in PageMill:

- Logical styles
- Physical styles

Logical styles are those that are assigned by the browser (in other words, how they appear depends on how the Web browser interprets the data). Types of Logical styles that you assign are:

- **Strong**
- *Emphasis*
- *Citation*
- *Sample*
- Keyboard
- Teletype
- Code
- Variable

(Logical styles are shown here in the style that PageMill will use.) In practice, Logical styles have not been very popular with Webpublishers because it is impossible to know how a browser will interpret them.

Physical styles are assigned by the literal application of style, all browsers will interpret them in the same manner. Types of Physical styles include bold and italic.

To assign a certain style to text, highlight the text to which you want to apply the style, then choose a style from the Style menu (see Figure 2.8). Try combining styles with headings to create interesting heading effects.

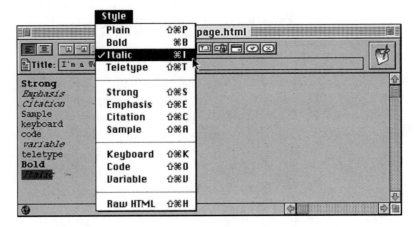

Figure 2.8
Assign a style to
your text.

Rules

Adding a horizontal rule to your Web page is an excellent way to break up text and add a graphic element to your page. To add a horizontal rule to your text, click the Insert Horizontal Rule button in the tool bar (see Figure 2.9). By default, the rule stretches across the page and is left justified.

Figure 2.9
Click the Insert
Horizontal Rule
button to create a
horizontal rule.

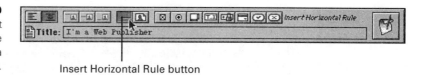

Insert Horizontal Rule button

To manipulate the size and appearance of the horizontal rule, place the cursor on the horizontal rule so that the cursor turns from a cross-hair into an arrow. Now click the horizontal rule. An outline appears around the rule (see Figure 2.10). Notice the dark boxes at the lower right, far right, and lower middle of the outline. These dark boxes are sizing handles that enable you to adjust the width and thickness of the rule.

Figure 2.10
Preparing to resize
a horizontal rule.

sizing handle

To resize the width of the rule, click the far right handle and drag it to the left. To resize the thickness of the rule, click the lower middle handle and drag down. To resize the thickness and width of the rule at the same time (see Figure 2.11), click the lower right rule and drag down (or up) and to the left (or right).

You also can control whether the rule is left justified or centered by selecting the rule and clicking the tool bar's alignment buttons. These buttons are discussed in the next section.

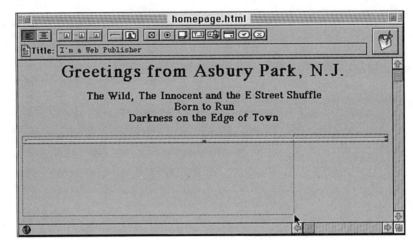

Figure 2.11
Adjusting the width
and thickness of a
horizontal rule.

Tip

Rule width and thickness also can be adjusted with the Attributes Inspector. See Chapter 3 for details.

Aligning Text

PageMill provides control for both left and center alignment of text. Use the two buttons on the top left of the tool bar to adjust the alignment of text.

Note

PageMill does not offer right alignment even though there is a Netscape extension for one.

Aligning Text

1 Open a new PageMill document.

2 Type the following text into your new PageMill document:

Greetings from Asbury Park, N.J.

The Wild, The Innocent and the E Street Shuffle

Born to Run

Darkness on the Edge of Town

3 Highlight the text and select the Center Align Text button from the tool bar (see Figure 2.12).

Note

Graphics and rules can also be aligned in this manner.

Center Align button

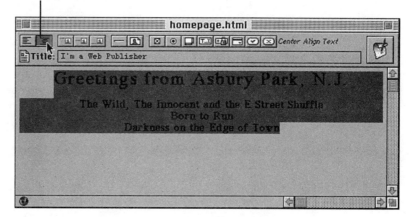

Figure 2.12
Center align text.

Creating Lists

Lists are commonly used in Web pages because they make a document easier to read. Use lists for describing items such as a table of contents, a series of steps, outlining a topic, and indexing. Lists combined with hypertext links create a powerful and orderly way to organize information on a Web page. You can create the following types of lists with PageMill:

- Bulleted

- Directory

- Menu

- Numbered

- Definition

- Term

Following are examples of how to create each list.

Bulleted Lists

Bulleted lists are used to present items that can be described briefly—usually in 10 words or less. In bulleted lists, each item in the list is preceded by a bullet(•). The appearance of the bullet is controlled by the font (and browser). Do not assume that your bullet will appear as a solid black circle on every browser.

Use your current PageMill document for the following tutorial.

Creating a Bulleted List

1 Type the following items (press Return after each word):

Writer

Lawyer

Beggarman

Thief

2 Now press Return and choose Paragraph from the Format menu.

3 Highlight everything you typed.

4 Select List from the Format menu and then choose Bullet (⌘-Opt-B) from the popup hierarchical menu (see Figure 2.13).

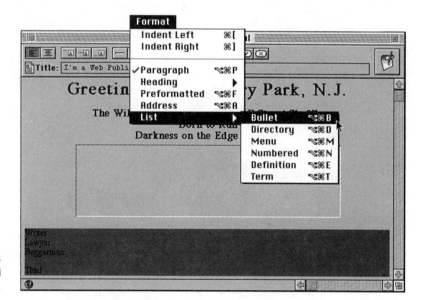

Figure 2.13
Creating a bulleted list.

Note

Heads-up all of you advanced HTMLers. The Paragraph command is not what you think. PageMill's Paragraph command generates a

 tag, *not* a <P> tag. This was a major concession made by the authors of PageMill to accommodate the way Netscape handles the <BR> tag.

This is where the worlds collide between using PageMill and writing your own HTML. Remember that what you do in PageMill is eventually generated into HTML commands. Therefore, it's a good idea to get into correct habits when using PageMill so that clean HTML is generated for you. Why do you care? Two reasons. Someone might need to edit your HTML someday and you want to make sure that you've left clean code. And, HTML browsers are likely to get more nitpicky about adherence to HTML standards as the Web becomes more complex. Getting into good habits with PageMill will ensure that your pages continue to be displayed correctly by future browsers.

The best way to generate lists is to type the list items, separate them by a Return, and end the list with a Return and a Paragraph command (⌘-Opt-P) after the last item.

Directory and Menu

Two other options for creating a bulleted list are included in the PageMill Lists menu: Directory and Menu. These commands function identically to the Bullet command. They were included as part of the HTML 1.0 and 2.0 specifications, and therefore are supported by PageMill. Menu and Directory are not included in the forthcoming HTML 3.0 specification. When you need to create an unordered list, it's best to stick with a numbered or definition and term list.

Numbered Lists

In numbered lists, each item begins with a numeral. Numbered lists are great for step-by-step instructions and ordered rankings.

 Creating a Numbered List

1 Type the following items (press Return after each name):

   Stephanie Marie

   Jillian Leigh

   Emma Leanne

   Terrie Jo

2 Now highlight everything you typed.

3 Select List from the Format menu and then select Numbered from the popup hierarchical menu.

4 Notice that PageMill inserts #. before each item while in Edit mode. When viewed by a browser, these characters are correctly translated into numbers.

PageMill can easily convert between numbered and bulleted lists. To do so, highlight the entire numbered list. Then select List from the Format menu and choose Bullet from the popup hierarchical menu. Voilà! To convert from a bulleted list to a numbered list, choose Numbered from the popup hierarchical menu.

Definition and Term Lists

These two list components work together. They are used to introduce a term and then provide a definition. The most common use of Definition and Term elements are glossaries. Instead of bullets or numbers preceding a term, the term is listed at the far left of the page. The definition component is indented.

Close all open PageMill windows and start a new PageMill document by selecting New Page from the File menu (⌘-N).

Creating a Definition/Term List

1 For this command summary, you will enter list terms and definitions. Press Return after each line.

Shovel

An excavating machine

Pot

A rounded or earthen container

Basket

A receptacle made of interwoven material

2 Highlight everything you typed.

3 Select List from the Format menu and then select Term from the popup hierarchical menu. Everything you just typed should now be styled Term.

4 Next, highlight a definition. Select List from the Format menu and then select Definition from the popup hierarchical menu. Repeat this for each of the definitions. Your document should now look like Figure 2.14.

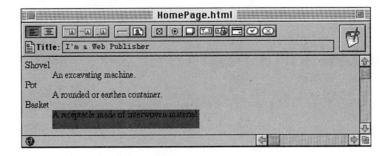

Figure 2.14
Creating a
Definition/Term list.

Do not close this PageMill document. You will use it in the next section to add graphics.

Adding Graphics

Graphic images make a Web site more appealing and professional looking. A picture really can be worth a thousand words when you're trying to convey information. In this section, you'll learn the various ways to get graphics into PageMill. Graphics also are presented in Chapter 4, "Imagemaps and the Image View." The images referred to throughout these lessons come with *The PageMill Handbook* CD-ROM. The images are located in the Images folder within the EarthAndWare Tutorials folder.

 Tip

Viewers can turn off automatic graphic loading on their browsers. You can enter a label for the graphic in the Attributes Inspector's Image mode Alt field so that viewers who turn off graphics will see a descriptive label instead of a blank space.

Drag-and-Drop

You can drag the icon of an image file from the Finder right into PageMill, and it will be inserted on your page.

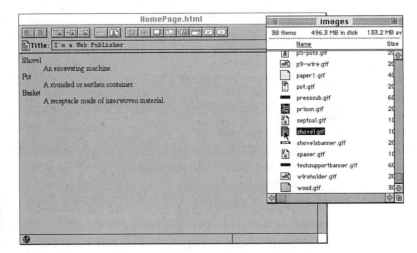

Figure 2.15
Drag the shovel.gif
file to the PageMill
window.

Dragging and Dropping an Image

1 Place the cursor at the end of the definition for shovel. Click to place the cursor.

2 Open the Images folder within the EarthAndWare Tutorials folder.

3 Find the file shovel.gif and drag it into the PageMill document (see Figure 2.15).

The preferred format for graphics on the Web is GIF. PageMill can automatically convert JPEG format graphics into GIF when you insert a graphic by dragging and dropping it onto a PageMill document (see Figure 2.16). The converted GIF file will be placed in the Images folder that you specified in the Preferences menu (discussed at the beginning of this chapter).

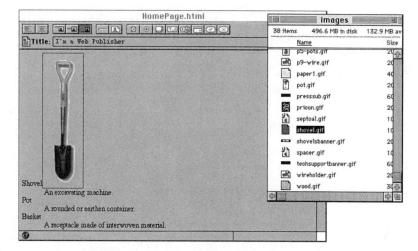

Figure 2.16
PageMill automatically places the image into your document.

Pasteboard

Images also can be stored on the Pasteboard for easy retrieval. The Pasteboard is a multipage clipboard that is part of the PageMill program. It can hold several images, text items, and hypertext links on the same page. Select Show Pasteboard (⌘-/) from the Window menu to access the Pasteboard. Items are moved to and from the Pasteboard via drag-and-drop (see Figure 2.17).

Images also can be pasted into PageMill from the Macintosh Clipboard.

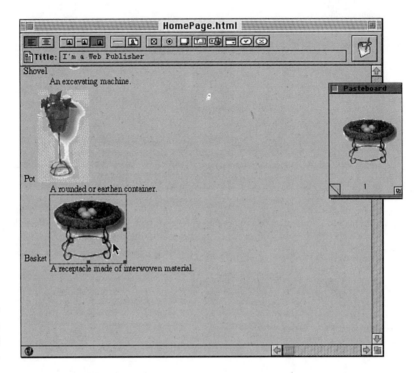

Figure 2.17
Dragging a file from
the Pasteboard into
your document.

Insert Image Button

You can use the Insert Image button, shown in Figure 2.18, to
initiate the placement of a graphic. The Insert Image button
presents you with a standard Macintosh file dialog box that you
can then use to identify the file you want to place.

Figure 2.18
The Insert Image
button on the
PageMill tool bar.

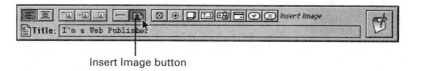

Insert Image button

Using the Insert Image Button

1 Place the cursor at the end of the definition for pot. Click to place the cursor.

2 Click the Insert Image button.

3 Find the file pot.gif in the Images folder within the EarthAndWare Tutorials folder and select it.

4 Click Open.

Figure 2.19 shows the dialog box used to insert a graphic using the Image button.

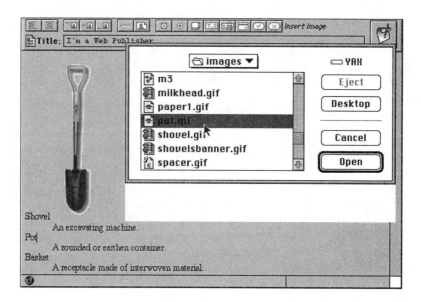

Figure 2.19
Choose the pot.gif
file. Place the image
on your home page.

Aligning Text to Images

When text is next to an image, you have some control over the alignment of the text. You can align the text to the bottom, middle, or top of the graphic.

Aligning Text to Images

1 Select the pot graphic by clicking it once.

2 Click the Top Align Text button in the tool bar. The definition text now will be aligned with the top of the pot graphic.

3 Click the Middle Align Text button in the tool bar. The definition text will now be aligned with the middle of the pot graphic.

Resizing Graphics

You can use two methods to resize a graphic:

- Drag the graphic to the size you desire

- Use the Attributes Inspector to enter precise dimensions for the graphic

Resizing a Graphic Using the Drag Method

1 Select the graphic you want to resize by clicking it once.

2 When selected, sizing handles appear (they should look like the sizing handles you used when resizing the horizontal rule). Click and drag these handles to size the image (see Figure 2.20).

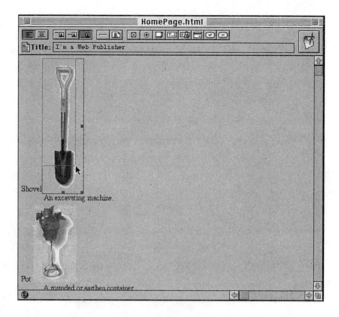

Figure 2.20
You can resize an
image simply by
dragging one of its
sizing handles.

Precise control over a graphic is provided in the Attributes Inspector. Using the Attributes Inspector you can:

- Control the width and height of the image in pixels or as a percent

- Specify the number of pixels to serve as a border around the image

- Create a text name for the image (for users who do not use graphics in their browsers)

- Specify if the image is to be used as a submit button for forms

- Specify if the image is to be used as a clickable imagemap

Resizing a Graphic Using the Image Mode of the Attributes Inspector

1 Select the image.

2 Invoke the Attributes Inspector (⌘-;) from the Window menu.

3 Make sure Scale to Height and Scale to Width are *not* selected.

4 Adjust the size of the image by changing the values in the width and height boxes (see Figure 2.21).

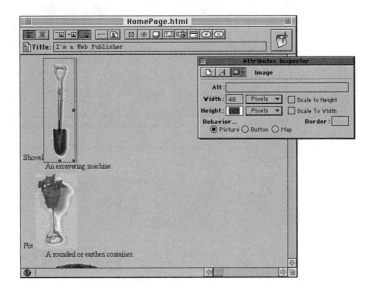

Figure 2.21
Using the Attributes Inspector to resize images.

Hypertext Links

Hypertext links are the heart and soul of the Web. Hypertext is based on the concept that text can be linked to other documents to reveal additional information. Both text and images can serve as linking points on the Web. With hypertext links, readers can navigate to:

■ Another part of the same Web page

■ Another Web page on your server

■ A page on another Web server

By default, the hypertext links you create appear underlined in blue text. Images that have links associated with them appear outlined in blue. In Preview mode, PageMill's cursor turns from an arrow to a pointing finger when it passes over a hypertext link.

URLs

URL stands for Uniform Resource Locator. A URL is a standard-ized way of accessing files on the Web. It is, in a sense, an address much like your street, city, state, country, and ZIP code. A URL has three parts:

■ The name of the Internet service (or protocol) being used; for example: `ftp`, `telnet`, `gopher`, `http`, and so on.

■ The domain name of the computer to be accessed (also called a *host*); for example: `www.mactivity.com`.

■ The directory path for the file to be viewed; for example: `/conferences/macweb.html`

When you put these together, you get `http://www.mactivity.com/conferences/macweb.html`

This particular address has been specified to use the `http` protocol to connect to the machine named `www.mactivity.com` and to find the file `macweb.html` in the `conferences` folder.

URL names cannot include any spaces, backslashes, or international characters because not all machines can interpret these characters. Remember not to use those marks when creating folders and documents that will be used on the Web.

You should know the following about URLs:

- The various notations and symbols of the technical world don't always fit into the concise rules of English. URL descriptions are a good example. When a sentence ends with a URL, you need to end the sentence with a period. URLs *never end in a period*—so ignore any periods at the end of sentences when typing URLs into your Web page or browser.

- The proper way to define a URL that attaches to a site is to end the hostname with a forward slash (/). When a Web server sees a slash at the end of a URL, it knows to serve a page that has been designated as a default page for that site. This is why when you tell someone to check out your Web site and give them a URL with just a machine name (that is, `www.mymachine.com`) they will see the default home page for that site.

Relative versus Absolute Pathnames

PageMill supports the use of relative pathnames to make hypertext links. A relative pathname describes the location of a document *relative* to the location of the current document. When creating a link to a document that is in the same folder as the document that will contain the hypertext link, you can simply specify the filename instead of the complete pathname.

By contrast, an *absolute* pathname describes the complete path from the root of the server to the file.

In general, it's a better idea to use relative pathnames. This way if you ever move your files and folders to another computer, the URLs still will be correct.

Creating a Hypertext Link

Several facilities are available for creating hypertext links in PageMill. You should keep two important concepts in mind when creating hypertext links. The first is the source text that will be used to jump to another location. By default this text appears underlined in blue in PageMill. The second concept is the destination or the place to which you are linking. The destination can be a position on the current page, the top of another page, or a position on another page, located locally on your server or somewhere out on the Web.

Drag-and-Drop Icons

Hypertext links are one of the areas in which PageMill's use of drag-and-drop really shines. You can drag-and-drop the Page, Anchor, and Image icons to create hypertext links. PageMill takes drag-and-drop a step further by maintaining relevant information. When you drag a PageMill link to the Pasteboard or among PageMill documents, PageMill retains the hypertext associations for that object.

Creating a Hypertext Link to Another Page

Use your PageMill document from the last exercise for this tutorial.

You must have full version of PageMill to complete this exercise. Remember, documents need to be saved for the Page icon to be available.

1 Open a new PageMill document by selecting New Page from the File menu (⌘-N). An untitled PageMill document will appear over your previous document.

2 Drag the Page icon from your first page and drop it onto the text area of your untitled PageMill document. A hypertext link to your first page appears (see Figure 2.22). Clicking the hypertext link in Preview mode or when the page is accessed by a browser will take users to the top of the page by default.

3 To create a hypertext link to another part of the same Web page, create an anchor by dragging the Page icon to the location you want to mark as an anchor. An Anchor icon is then visible.

4 Highlight the text you want to be the source hypertext link.

5 Drag the destination Anchor icon on top of the highlighted source text (see Figure 2.23).

If the source text and destination anchor are not visible on a single screen, use PageMill's autoscrolling feature to help create the hypertext link. A hot scrolling area is provided along the edges of each PageMill page. The autoscrolling region is a 16-pixel-wide border at the left, right, top, and bottom edges of the Page view. If you drag an item to this area and wait for a second, scrolling will begin. You also can use the Pasteboard as a temporary holding area for the anchor.

Clicking on the source hypertext link in the Preview mode will now take you to the location of your anchor.

 Tip

To name an anchor, select it, open the Attributes Inspector, and select the Object Attributes button. A name field appears that enables you to change the name of the anchor. Change the name and press Return. Be sure to rename your anchor *before* you start creating hypertext links with it.

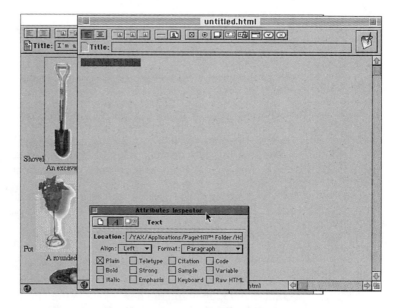

Figure 2.22
Dragging the Page
icon from one page
to another creates a
hypertext link.

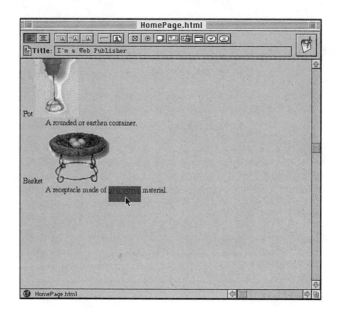

Figure 2.23
Dragging the Page
icon from within the
text creates a
hypertext link to the
same page.

Creating a Link to a Page on Another Site

1 Activate the Link Location bar by clicking in the gray area at the bottom of your PageMill document (to the right of the blue Globe icon). A white text area appears.

2 Enter the URL of the destination site in the Link Location field.

3 Use Anchors to identify locations within a Web page that you want to serve as link destinations. Create an anchor by dragging the Page icon onto the PageMill document. Link the Anchor to text by highlighting the text and then dragging and dropping the anchor on top of the highlighted text.

Tip

You can edit the name of the link in the source document. Simply highlight it and type the new name in the Link Location field.

Cutting and Pasting Links

Once a hypertext link is created, you can cut and paste a hypertext link to another area on your Web page or to another page. PageMill preserves the URL associated with the linked text when you cut and paste.

Tip

Drag any commonly used hypertext links to the Pasteboard for easy access when creating other pages. Dragging places a copy of the hypertext link, with associated URL intact, onto the Pasteboard. You can then Option-drag from the Pasteboard into the new page. Option-dragging from the Pasteboard places a copy of the hypertext link on your page.

Deleting a Link

You can remove a hypertext link from your document using one of the following two ways:

- Delete the text that represents a hypertext link

- Highlight the text that represents a hypertext link and select Remove Link (⌘-R) from the Edit menu

 Tip

Triple-clicking a link selects the link and displays the URL destination in the Link Location bar.

You also can move a copy of linked text to a new location by selecting the text and Option-dragging it to a new location. The link will now appear in both places.

Testing Your Links

PageMill's Preview mode supports testing of local hypertext links—hypertext links to documents that are on your computer. To test links, make sure PageMill is in Preview mode.

When you place the cursor on top of text or graphics that have a hypertext link associated with them, the cursor changes from an arrow to a pointed finger. When you select a hypertext link that links to another page, the other page launches on top of your existing page.

 Note

PageMill does not support testing links to URLs on the Internet.

Creating Forms

PageMill provides a powerful and easy facility for creating and manipulating form elements on a Web page. Forms can be used to do many things, including the following:

- Receive feedback from the people who browse your page

- Search a database

- Collect data

For a form to be useful, however, a Web server needs a special application, called a CGI, to help with the processing of the information. (CGIs are discussed more thoroughly in Chapter 5.)

For the purposes of this section, all you need to understand is that a CGI is needed to interact with the form data—whether it's writing the data to a database such as Claris FileMaker Pro, ACIUS 4th Dimension, or Everywhere Developement's Butler, or returning information based on the form data. PageMill only presents the form. Acting on the data is the job of a CGI.

To create a form, click one of the form element buttons in the tool bar (see Figure 2.24). Form elements can be modified and edited for your specific needs.

Insert form elements

Figure 2.24
Click on a form
element to activate
it in your document.

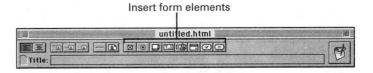

Form Elements

Web page form elements can be classified into three categories:

- Fields
- Popup menus
- Buttons

Fields

Fields are form elements into which users enter text. PageMill provides three types of fields:

- Text Fields
- Text Areas
- Password Fields

Text Fields are single-line fields that can be modified by width only (see Figure 2.25). Text Areas are multiple-line fields that can be modified by width and height (see Figure 2.25). Password Fields are a special type of text field. When a viewer types text into a Password Field, bullets appear in place of the actual text being typed (see Figure 2.25).

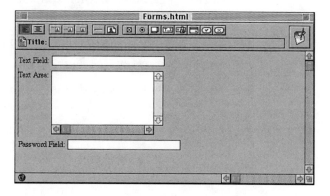

Figure 2.25
Allowing users to give feedback through forms.

Menus

Menus are form elements in which users select from a list of choices. PageMill supports the use of customizable popup menus (see Figure 2.26).

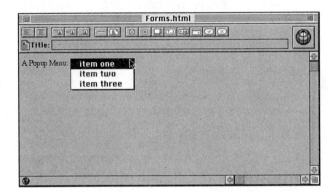

Figure 2.26
Selecting from a popup menu.

Buttons

Buttons are form elements in which users use their mouse to make selections or to take action. PageMill provides the following types of buttons:

- Radio buttons are used when you want users to select only one item from a list (see Figure 2.27).

- Checkboxes are used when you want users to be able to select multiple items from a list (see Figure 2.27).

- The Submit button is used to send the data collected on a form to the server (see Figure 2.27).

- The Reset button is used to give users an opportunity to reset or clear their choices before submitting their data (see Figure 2.27).

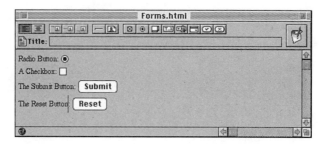

Figure 2.27
Examples of four
different form
buttons.

Creating a Form

1 Before you begin building your form, create a new page in PageMill.

2 Type **Name**: and press the Spacebar.

3 Click the Insert Text Field button on the tool bar, and press Return.
   Press Return.

4 Type **Password**: and press the Spacebar.

5 Click the Insert Password Field button on the tool bar, and press Return.

6 Type **Street Address:** and press the Spacebar.

7 Click the Insert Text Field button on the tool bar, and press Return.

8 Type **City:** and press the Spacebar.

9 Click the Insert Text Field button on the tool bar, and press Return.

10 Type **State:** and press the Spacebar.

11 Click the Insert Text Field button on the tool bar, and press Return.

12 Type **Country:** and press the Spacebar.

13 Click the Insert Text Field button on the tool bar, and press Return.

14 Type **Zip**: and press the Spacebar.

15 Click the Insert Text Field button on the tool bar, and press Return.

16 Type **Tell us about yourself**: and press the Spacebar.

17 Click on the Insert Text Area icon from the tool bar, and press Return.

Your completed document should look like Figure 2.28.

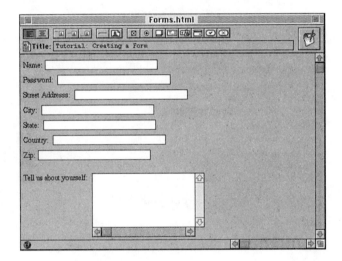

Figure 2.28
Creating forms with
PageMill.

 Tip

Insert text inside a field to give a hint to the reader what he or she should type into the field. To do this, enter the text into the field when you create it. Inside the Name field, for example, you could type **Enter name here**. The text will be presented to every reader who loads the form.

Modifying Form Elements

1 Adjust the length of Text Fields and Password Fields by clicking once in the field and dragging the sizing handle located on the far-right sides of the field.

2 Adjust the length and width of Text Areas by clicking once in the field and dragging the sizing handles on the bottom-middle, bottom-right, and far-right sides of the field.

Tip

Drag frequently-used form elements to the Pasteboard for easy access when designing other Web pages.

Using Radio Buttons

1 Type **Select your gender:** and press Return.

2 Type **Male:** and click the Insert Radio Button button on the tool bar.

3 Press the Spacebar three times.

4 Type **Female:** Clone the radio button that you previously created by selecting it and then holding down the Option key as you drag it to the right of the Female descriptive tag.

5 Deselect button and press Return.

Your document now should look like Figure 2.29.

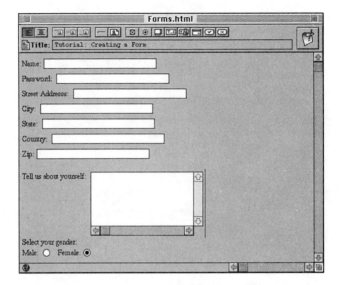

Figure 2.29
Be sure to clone
your radio buttons.

Radio buttons need to be created as a group to work properly. The first button must be created by selecting the Insert Radio button from the tool bar. Subsequent buttons for the group must be created by cloning the original button.

You can clone radio buttons three ways. The first method is to select the original button and copy and paste it to subsequent locations. The second method is to Option-drag the original to subsequent locations. Option-dragging creates a copy of the original button. The third method for creating buttons as a group is to create the individual buttons by selecting the Insert Radio button from the tool bar. To clone them, select each of the buttons, go to the Attributes Inspector, select Object Attributes (icon on the far right) and give each of the buttons the same name.

Using Checkboxes

1 Type **Which of the following do you own:** and press Return.

2 Type **Stereo** and press Return.

3 Type **TV** and press Return.

4 Type **VCR** and press Return.

5 Place the cursor next to Stereo, and click the Insert Checkbox button on the tool bar.

6 Place the cursor next to TV, and click the Insert Checkbox button on the tool bar.

7 Place the cursor next to VCR, and click the Insert Checkbox button on the tool bar, and press Return.

Tip

To create forms in which the form elements align neatly, use the Teletype style for the descriptive tags and add spaces after the tags to align them. Using the Teletype style ensures that a monospaced type font is used so that spacing is even. This will give your forms a clean, professional look. Try it.

Select all the elements of your form input area including the descriptive tags. Select the Teletype style from the Style menu. Manually add spaces between the descriptive tags and the text fields to line them up. Your document should now look like Figure 2.30.

Figure 2.30
Using the Teletype
style, you can
manually add
spaces to your list
to ensure that your
checkboxes line up
correctly.

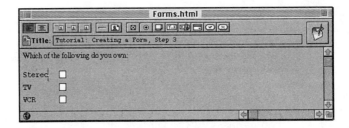

Using Popup

1 Type **Select Income Bracket** Menus.

2 Click the Insert Popup on the tool bar.

3 Double-click the Popup menu that appears. You'll see item one, item two, and item three as default selections in the popup.

4 Highlight Item 1 and type **$20,000–$50,000** (notice the field width widens to accommodate the length of the text).

5 Highlight Item 2 and type **$50,001–100,000**.

6 Highlight Item 3 and type **$100,001–$500,000**.

7 Add a fourth item to the list by pressing the Return key, and typing **+$500,000**.

Your popup menu should now look like Figure 2.31.

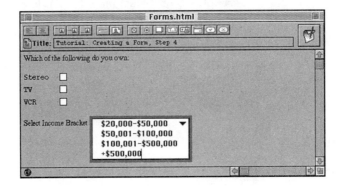

Figure 2.31
Creating a popup
menu.

A few things you should know about popup menus:

- Popups can have as many items in them as you choose.

- You can select the default item by sliding the inverted triangle in the list next to the item you want to be the default.

- You can determine whether the popup is open all the time by sizing the popup while in Edit mode. To size the popup, select it once and drag the sizing handle at the bottom of the popup down until all menu items are visible.

- Using the Attributes Inspector, you can specify how many items can be seen before the list is opened.

- Using the Attributes Inspector, you can determine if viewers can select multiple items in the list. Specifying this option places checkboxes next to each item in the list.

The Address Tag

Logistical information about a Web site usually is at the bottom of the Web page. This information might include copyright information, how to contact the Webpublisher, and the date that the document was last updated. This section is referred to as the address or signature and typically is set off from the main body by a horizontal rule.

 Using the Address Tag

1 If you haven't already done so, create a horizontal rule to separate the body of your Web page from the bottom, and press Return.

2 Type **Copyright 1995 Webs-R-US** and press Return.

3 Type your email address in the format **yourname@yourhost.domain** (for example, paul@mactivity.com) and press Return.

4 Type **Last Updated, December 1, 1995,** and press Return.

5 Highlight the text.

6 Select Address from the Format menu. The text now appears italicized.

PageMill can create a special type of hypertext link for your email address that instructs mail-capable browsers to open a mail window, with the send to address already filled in.

Creating a MailTo: Link

1 Highlight your email address.

2 Click in the Link Location bar.

3 Type the URL: **mailto:yourname@yourhost.domain,** press Return.

The text now appears underlined in blue, because it is a special type of hypertext link (see Figure 2.32). The PageMill Preview mode is not a mail-capable browser, so you can't test this functionality from PageMill. You can, however, test this functionality from Netscape.

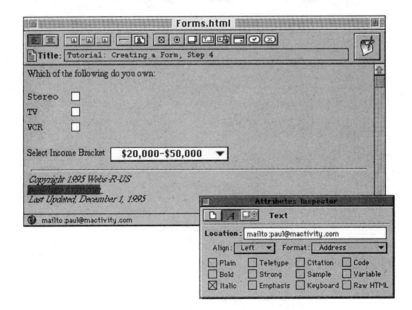

Figure 2.32
Creating a MailTo link on your home page.

Summary

This chapter covered the basic functionality of PageMill and introduced you to many of PageMill's advanced features. You should now be able to create basic Web pages and put them on the Web. Take it a step further and explore PageMill's advanced features and learn how to take complete control of your Web pages. All this begins in the next chapter.

Chapter 3

Using the Attributes Inspector

The Attributes Inspector is PageMill's primary control panel. You can use it to control just about every element of your Web page. The Attributes Inspector is very powerful, and provides an alternative to menu commands and dialog boxes for many operations. This chapter discusses the information you need to know to effectively use the Attributes Inspector.

The Attributes Inspector handles four major tasks:

- Changing background and foreground colors
- Changing the style of text
- Adjusting the size and behavior of images
- Building fill-in forms

Opening the Attributes Inspector

 Note

The Attributes Inspector is a floating palette that remains open and active while you are working on a document.

Open a new document. Select Show Attributes Inspector from the Window menu. Alternatively, you can show and hide the Attributes Inspector by pressing ⌘-;. The Attributes Inspector will appear as shown in Figure 3.1.

 Tip

The Attributes Inspector remains open, but is not active when the document is in Preview mode. If the Attributes Inspector doesn't seem to be working, make sure your document is in Edit mode.

Figure 3.1
The Attributes
Inspector.

Page Mode

Page mode is used to adjust attributes relating to the entire document. To activate Page mode, select the page icon from the top left of the Attributes Inspector. The box at the top of the Inspector is called Action, and next to it is a pull-down menu with two options: Get and Post.

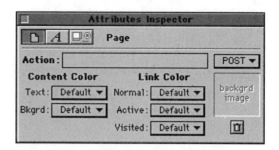

Figure 3.2
Post option.

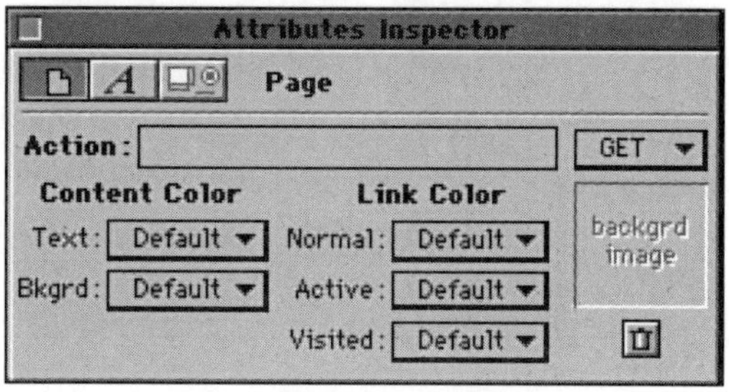

Figure 3.3
Get option.

The Get and Post functions and the Action box are used with fill-in forms—special pages that allow viewers visiting your Web site to enter information and send it to the server. Get, Post, and the Action box determine how the form's information is processed and to what part of the server it is sent.

Fill-in forms are a big subject, and one that will be discussed later in this chapter. For now, however, let's get to some of the other features of Page mode: content color, link color, and background image.

Text Color

In the Attributes Inspector, you can adjust the color of both the text and the background. You can make these any color you like, but you can only set these colors once per page. This is a limitation of all Web pages (even those built without the help of PageMill). You can't have a page that has orange text for one paragraph, and then a list with purple text. Likewise, the top half of your page can't have a green background and the bottom half a white background. This is a "feature" of HTML and, because the final product of PageMill is an HTML file, you have to follow its rules.

Changing Text Color

With Page mode active in the Attributes Inspector, select Custom on the Text popup menu. The standard Apple Color Wheel window appears.

Click the desired color in the circle.

Click OK.

Click the slider at the bottom of the window adjust the lightness, which ranges from 0 percent (black) to 100 percent (white). Slide the slider back and forth and notice that the number in the Lightness window moves with it. Stop at about 30 percent. Look at the square in the upper-right corner. The top half shows the color your page currently is using. The bottom half displays the new color you are creating as you move the sliders.

Hue angle and saturation also can be adjusted by typing new numbers in the windows or by moving the cross-hairs in the center of the circle. Click the cross-hairs and move them toward the 0 degree mark. Stop when you almost reach the edge. You should get a nice dark red color. Click OK, go back to your document window, and type some text in the new color.

Note

Remember that you can only set text color once per page, so make sure that this is a color that works well within your page design.

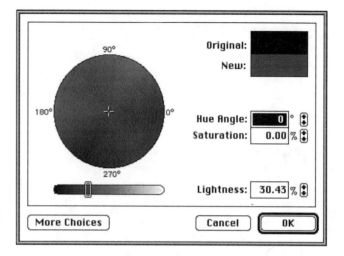

Figure 3.4
Custom Color
Wheel.

A button located in the lower left of this window offers you more choices. Click the More Choices button and a column appears on the left side of the window called Apple HSL, which is the official name for this color wheel (HSL stands for Hue/Saturation/ Lightness). You can also generate colors by specifying percentages of red, green, and blue. To do this, click the option for Apple RGB. The Apple RGB panel doesn't really offer more choices; it provides another way to choose the same colors by using sliders that adjust the intensity of the reds, greens, and blues. Slide the sliders down to 0% and you get black. Slide them up to 100% and you get white. You also can type the values of red, green, and blue into the spaces to the left of the sliders.

 Note

PageMill translates color into qualities of red, green, and blue when it outputs to HTML, because browsers only understand colors as combinations of red, green, and blue.

Using the Apple RGB panel is helpful if you know the RGB qualities of a certain color (for instance, you found the color in another application such as Photoshop) and want to replicate it. Otherwise, stick with the HSL panel. It is much easier to pick colors by dragging the cross-hairs around until you find the one you want.

Background Color

Using PageMill, you can also change background color of your page (the color of the window displayed to the viewer). Background color is changed by the same procedure used to change text color (see previous section).

Changing Text Color

1 In the Page mode of the Attributes Inspector, choose Custom on the Bkgrd popup menu. The standard Apple Color Wheel window appears.

2 Click the desired color.

3 Click OK.

A Web page's default background color is light gray. Click the cross-hairs in the Apple HSL Color Wheel, pull them to the left and down (toward seven o'clock, if this were a clock), and move the intensity slider down until you have a dark blue. Click OK and take a look at your document window.

To revert back to the original color of the background or the text, simply click the popup menu in the Attributes Inspector's Page mode that you used to change the colors to custom. Select the default option.

Background Images

Sure, changing the color of your background is cool, but that's only the beginning. With PageMill, you also can use an image, tiled in the background, to create a watermark effect for the background of your document.

In the Images folder of the EarthandWareTutorial Folder, find the file called paper1.gif. (When you do this, arrange the windows on your screen so that you can see the Attributes Inspector). Click paper1.gif and drag it onto the Attributes Inspector into the square with the words backgrd image.

Figure 3.5
Background
Images.

FYI

What's a GIF?

On any computer (not just a Macintosh), images are saved in one of a dozen formats. Images on the Macintosh, for example, are frequently saved in the TIFF or PICT format.

The preferable format on Web pages is GIF, and for a really good reason. GIF is the lowest common denominator of graphics formats. Every browser capable of displaying images (regardless of platform) is capable of displaying images saved in the GIF format.

The paper1.gif file is about 96 pixels wide and 96 pixels high. When you drag this file onto the Attributes Inspector, a few things happen. First, the Attributes Inspector checks to make sure that the file is a GIF. If it's in any other format, PageMill automatically converts it to GIF format. Next, PageMill tiles the image across the background of your document. Because paper1.gif is relatively small, it gets tiled quite a few times across the background. Lastly, a new file is created from background.gif and saved in the Images folder (created automatically by PageMill).

Note

If you are working in the window where you changed the background color, you'll notice that the image that you dragged to the Attributes Inspector has completely covered the background color. PageMill tiles background images so that they fit perfectly with the background and dynamically change to fit the size of browser windows. The background won't show through unless the background is transparent.

To delete a background image, click the small garbage can icon beneath the image in the lower-right corner of the Attributes Inspector. Your old background will return, including any color adjustments that you might have made.

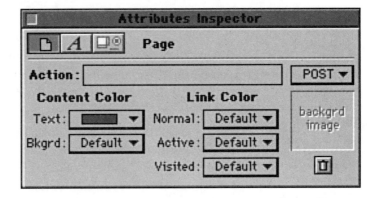

Figure 3.6
Garbage can icon.

Hypertext Link Colors

Previously, you read that the color of the text could be adjusted only once per document. However, this is not completely true. You can adjust the color of the text designated as hypertext links.

Three types of hypertext links are available:

Watermark effect
To create a watermark effect, where only one large image is in the background, create an image in your drawing program about 600 pixels wide and 600 pixels high. When you drag that image to the Attributes Inspector, PageMill will only have room to put the image in the background once. It won't have enough room to tile it more than once. The next copy of the image will appear directly below it.

■ Normal: Hypertext links that have not yet been explored

■ Active: Hypertext links that have been selected

■ Visited: Hypertext links that have been explored

Changing the color of links is not something you should do without a little thought. Most browsers display normal (unvisited) links in blue text, active links in red, and visited links in purple. This means that when you come to a new Web page, you see blue links. These are normal (unvisited) links that have not yet been explored. When you click a blue link, it becomes active and turns to red (links are only active while the mouse button is down). If you return to a page, the link is visited and is displayed in purple. Most users have come to expect links to be displayed in these colors.

If you create a page where all normal links are displayed in red, you run the risk of someone visiting your page and thinking that they have already been there. Or, if your visited links are displayed in blue, users will think that it is new information. So, as a rule, if you are going to change link colors, you should change all three types, and choose colors that are different from the three default colors. For example, make normal links yellow, active links green, and visited links aqua.

Adjusting Hypertext Link Colors

To adjust the hypertext link colors, find Normal, Active, or Visited under the Link Color heading. In the Page mode of the Attributes Inspector, select Custom from the pull-down menu next to each and adjust the colors.

First adjust the Normal links color to yellow. In the Apple HSL panel, bring the cross-hairs to the upper right of the wheel (about two o'clock), and click OK. Now adjust the colors of the other links.

Because the Active link's default color is red, and red is similar to the color of the regular text, the link color should be green. Move the cross-hairs to the upper left of the color wheel (about 11 o'clock), and click OK.

Lastly, adjust the Visited link color. You already used red, yellow, blue, and green. To really make Visited links stand out, make them black. Drag the slider located at the bottom of the window all the way to the left. This turns the entire wheel black, so it doesn't matter where the cross-hairs are. Click OK.

Now, in your document window, create a link to a file called `link.html` by typing **link.html** in the Link Location bar. The text that you designate as a link should turn yellow. When the link becomes Active, it will turn green, and when it is Visited, it will turn black.

 Note

If you don't remember how to create a link, refer to Chapter 2.

Building a Fill-in Form

Fill-in forms are special kinds of Web pages (or parts of pages) that enable the person browsing your site to enter information and send it back to the server. Examples of fill-in forms include: order forms for products or feedback forms to find out what people think about your site or a particular subject.

The actual form that the viewer sees, with fields to input text or choose one of three options, is built using the tool bar at the top of the PageMill window. Chapter 2 describes how to use these buttons to create the form and move the elements, but these concepts will be reviewed here as well. In this section, you will build a form that asks users about their travel habits.

So, if you create the form in the main PageMill window (in Edit mode), what do you do with the Attributes Inspector? Three things:

■ Designate the CGI that handles the form's information. Remember, CGIs (Common Gateway Interfaces) are small applications that extend the functionality of your Web site.

■ Specify how the server should process the information it receives from this form (whether it needs to get information or post information).

■ Name the fields into which the user will enter information.

Get/Post and Action

At the top of the Attributes Inspector's Page mode are the Action field and the Get/Post pull-down menu. These are probably the most technical aspects of PageMill and deal with the process of serving the document. Before you grab your Webmaster caps, however, go back to the Edit mode of PageMill and create a fill-in form.

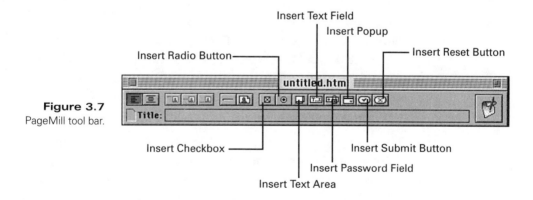

Figure 3.7
PageMill tool bar.

Creating a Fill-in Form

1 Click the Insert Text Field button once and press Return.

2 Click the Insert Text Area button once and press Return.

3 Click the Insert Password Field button once and press Return.

4 Click the Insert Popup button once and press Return.

5 Click the Insert Radio Button button seven times pressing Return.

6 Click the Insert Checkbox button seven times pressing Return after each insertion.

Now you have a place where viewers can input text. While this is definitely a good thing, it is only part of the process used to create forms. You need a way to send the information in these forms to the Web server. A form that has been filled out and not sent to the server isn't much good to anyone.

This is where Get/Post and Action come into the picture. For Web servers to do anything with information that a viewer has input into a form (like put it into a database, for example), the form information must be sent to a CGI (Common Gateway Interface) that can manipulate the data. In the Action field, you specify the CGI to which you want to send the form information. This is done with a Universal Resource Locator (URL). In the Action field, type the URL of the CGI that is going to handle the data coming from this form. If you are using a Macintosh Web server, a number of CGI options are explored in Chapter 5. For now, just put the datacapture.acgi in the Action field.

The Get/Post popup menu is a little more complex. Essentially, there are two different methods that servers and CGIs use to process data from a form. These are Get and Post. Think of Get as the method used when the server retrieves data, and Post as the method used when the server places data somewhere on the server.

Note

Most of the CGIs in Chapter 5 use the Post method.

Talking with the Webmaster

If you are working with a Webmaster who is going to handle the technical details of data coming in to the server from a form, you'll need to talk to him about the name of the CGI and the method that you should use (Get or Post).

Naming the Fields

The second part of building fill-in forms is naming the fields. If you have a field that asks the viewer for her email address, name that field something like **email**. When this information is sent to the server, it will look like this:

email=lisa@mactivity.com

This is the process of declaring variables and assigning values to them. Creating fill-in forms needs a little programming know-how, but PageMill provides a straight-forward interface.

Talking with the Webmaster

Again, if you are working with a Webmaster who's going to do the background techie stuff, you might need to talk to her about naming your fields. You might have to give the fields in your Web page the same names as she has given her fields in the database where the data will eventually go.

Let's have a quick computer science lesson to understand declaring variables. Variables are vitally important to just about every computer application ever created. The best way to think about variables is to imagine them as containers for data. If you've ever taken a basic algebra class, you've seen this in equations like this:

$x = 4$

$8 \div x = 2$

The x is the variable with a value of 4. After you've given it that value, you can use it in various ways, such as dividing 8 by it. Why is this better than simply stating $8 \div 2$? Because the value of x can be changed easily to get a different answer. For example:

$x = 2$

$8 \div x = 4$

This is a simple example, but if this were one of those horrible word problems, the need for variables would be more apparent. Forgive us for taking you back to the ninth grade for this next example.

Francine has 8 friends and 16 apples. How many apples will each friend get if she divides them equally? What if she has 24 apples?

$x = 16$

$x \div 8 = 2$

$x = 24$

$x \div 8 = 3$

In this example, x is equal to the number of friends that Francine has. The value of x can be changed easily to get different answers to the same question.

Computers can do this and much more with variables. In this case, you want to assign a user's input to a variable. So, if the variable x contains the data that a user entered for his or her name, a mechanism of telling the computer is needed:

$x = $ Joe User

You are not restricted to using only letters for variables. You can create a variable that looks like this:

name = Joe User

The server can do several things with this little piece of information, and it lets you keep track of the data. Later, this book will take a look at some of the things you can do with that data. First, let's see how to use PageMill to assign user input to variables.

The Forms Mode

Now let's go about naming the fields (also known as declaring variables) in the quick sample form. In the fill-in form you created at the beginning of this section, find the Text field in the document window (the long, single line field) and click it once to select it. Then click the third button from the left at the top of the Attributes Inspector (the one with the small text field and radio button on it). The words "Text Field" should appear at the top of the Inspector (if they don't, make sure that you have selected the text field in the document window).

In the Attributes Inspector, the word "Name" appears in bold next to the field that has the word "name" in it. Double-click in the text field to highlight the text, type **FirstName**, and press Return. This assigns the data entered into that field to the variable called "FirstName." After you press Return, the field should turn gray, which is PageMill's way of telling you that the name has been assigned to the field.

You can do two other things in this panel of the Attributes Inspector:

■ Change the size of the field

■ Set the maximum number of characters to be input

The default size is 30 characters, but you can make this larger or smaller by entering a different number in the "Size" box. To make the field larger, for example, type **45** in the field, and press Return. The user can now enter up to 45 characters in the field.

Let's do the same thing for the Password field and the Text area. Select the Password field. You should see the same window that you saw for the Text field. Click the Name field, type **password**, and press Return. Set the size of the field by typing **45** into the size field and pressing Return.

Now select the Text area. The only difference is that Size and Max Size have been replaced by Rows and Columns. Before you adjust these, assign this Text field to the variable **comments**. Click once in the Name field, type the variable name **comments**, and press Return.

You can change the size of the Text field by replacing the row and column numbers, by clicking a corner of the Text field and dragging it. The default size of the Text field is 7 rows by 27 columns. Change this to 5 rows by 45 columns so that this field lines up with the Text fields. Remember to press Return after you type the new numbers.

Text fields, text areas, and password fields are the simplest input types available. Essentially, you're creating a container, naming it (or assigning a variable to the information that will be placed in the container), and letting users dump in anything they want. This is perfect if you are asking a user for his or her name, or for comments.

Sometimes, though, you might want a user to select items from a list. Say, for example, you want to know if a user lives inside or outside the United States (a useful bit of information, because people from all over the planet will be looking at your work). You could include an input field and hope that he types "inside" or "outside." But what happens if he types "cold cuts"?

The solution is to give users a list and allow them to make selections only from that list. On the Web, there are two types of lists that you can present: those from which the user can choose one or more options (popup menus), and those from which the user can choose only one option (radio buttons).

Multiple Options Lists

Let's take the example already mentioned and make it slightly more complex. Let's say that you want to know what continent the user is on. You need to present seven choices and prevent someone from entering "cold cuts." Because the user can only be on one continent, he should be able to choose only one option from your list.

The easiest way to do this is with a popup menu. Think of popup menus as standard text fields with several options available. If you use a Macintosh (if you've made it this far in the book, you better), you are familiar with the concept of popup menus. Every item in the Macintosh menu bar is a popup menu.

 Note

Popup menus are also called pull-down menus.

Think about the standard File pull-down menu in the menu bar. When you hold down the mouse button on the word File a pull-down menu appears with the functions that you can perform. When you move the mouse to the command you want to select, a message is sent to Print, Save, Close, Quit, or whatever function you select. Imagine if the pull-down menu were replaced with a text field and you had to type Print in the field when you wanted to print. After the computer ignored your command for the third time because you made a typo, you'd be longing for the carefree elegance of Unix.

With PageMill, you can create the same user-friendly atmosphere on your Web page. Select the popup menu you created previously. Double-click the pop up menu and three options appear: item 1, item 2, and item 3. Highlight the items, and press Delete so that you can start clean. Enter the names of each continent and press Return after each entry. When you finish, click once elsewhere on the page, so that PageMill knows that you have finished putting options into your popup. You now have several pre-set options that can be placed into this field.

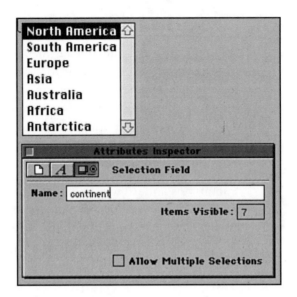

Figure 3.8
The continents.

Now you need to give this variable a name. Click the popup menu once and then click the button on the far right of the Attributes Inspector. Click in the Name field and type **continent**. Press Return after naming the field to save the variable name.

Two more options are on this screen: Items Visible and Allow Multiple Selections. To keep this a true popup menu (where only one item is displayed until the menu is selected, and then only one option can be selected from the list), leave both of these options empty. We'll come back to them later.

To test your popup menu, go to the Preview mode by clicking the icon in the upper-right corner of the page screen. Place the pointer on the popup menu and press the mouse button. All of the options appear. You can highlight each option by moving the mouse up and down the menu. Release the mouse button on one of the options, and the popup menu disappears leaving the option you selected as the one that is shown.

Radio Buttons

Another way to offer one and only one option from a list is to use radio buttons. Radio buttons are named after the preset buttons on radios. Think about the radio in your car. You can't be tuned to separate radio stations at the same time on the same radio, right? A mechanism allows you to go from the rock station to the jazz station, and not have both stations going at the same time. If you're listening to the rock station, which is preset on button #1, and want to flip to the jazz station, which is preset on button #2, you press button #2, which turns off button #1 and switches your radio to the jazz station.

To build a radio button into your Web page with PageMill you need a little variable trickery. Return to the seven radio buttons you created previously. You should have a row of seven radio buttons (see Figure 3.9).

Figure 3.9
Radio buttons.

Now, place the insertion point next to the first radio button and type **North America**. Continue typing until a continent name is next to each radio button. Your page should look like Figure 3.10.

Figure 3.10
Named radio
buttons.

Now you need to determine what each one of these buttons means. As you go into this, remember that you are offering several different responses to one question. If you think about this in terms of variables, you are offering several different pieces (each continent is a piece) that can be put into your container.

Click the first radio button, and then click the far right button in the Attributes Inspector. You should get a screen that gives you two fields: Name and Value. The Name field will have something cryptic in it like radio206506. Highlight this, and press Delete to clear it. Name this field **continent**. (And don't forget to press Return after you name the field.) Click in the Value field and type **North America**. Press Return.

Now click the next radio button. The Name field should change to another cryptic name. Click in this field, highlight the name and press Delete. Type the word **continent** in this field exactly as you did before. Now click in the Value field. Highlight the text in the field, and press Delete to clear it. Type **South America** to give this radio button a different value and press Return to lock in the value.

Go to Preview mode by clicking the button in the top right of the page screen. Click the radio button to the left of North America. Now click the radio button to the left of South America. If you built the buttons correctly, they'll toggle back and forth, just like your car radio. To put this another way, there are two options that assign different values to the same variable. Because this variable can only hold one value, when it gets a new one, it tosses the old one out.

Go back to the Edit mode. Click the other radio buttons and type **continent** in the Name field (back in the Attributes Inspector) and type a value that matches the text that you typed next to it in the main PageMill window. Each radio button should have the name continent, but a different value (make sure that you spell "continent" correctly for each radio button). When you have finished, go to the Preview mode and click any of the seven options, turning off the others.

Multiple Selections

Let's say that you want users to tell you which continents they have visited. You still want them to choose from the list that you established, but you want them to choose as many continents as they want. You can do this two different ways in PageMill.

In the previous examples, variables were described as containers for data. The data fit perfectly inside the container, leaving no room for anything else. For example, $x = 4$ or $x =$ Joe.

This is totally unacceptable for the task before us. To put several values into one variable, you need to author a document with a variable in it that will make room for as many items as the viewer wants to enter.

Go back to the Continents popup menu that you created earlier. Single-click to select it (make sure you're in Edit mode), and then click the third button to the right in the Attributes Inspector. Click the Allow Multiple Selections box at the bottom of the window.

Figure 3.11
Popup menu.

In Preview mode, you will find that your popup menu is no longer a popup. Click one of the options; it becomes highlighted. Now click another; it becomes highlighted, turning off the previous selection. No difference, right? Now hold down the Shift key and click a few of the options. You can select several options. Your popup menu looks like Figure 3.11.

If you go back into the Edit mode and return to the Attributes Inspector, there is a box in the third screen called the Selection Field that enables you to enter the number of options that you want to be visible. This is especially useful if you have a long list of options. You can make just a few options visible and let the user scroll through the list. For example, enter 4 in this box and press Return. Now only 4 continents are visible at a time in the popup menu.

Checkboxes

The other way to offer a user multiple options is with checkboxes. Checkboxes are a lot like radio buttons, but they do not cancel each other out when one is clicked.

Let's use the continent example one last time (I promise). Return to the seven checkboxes you created earlier. Type a continent name next to each of the checkboxes.

Select the first checkbox by single-clicking it. In the Attributes Inspector, click the third button. The screen that appears should be familiar to you; it is identical to the radio buttons screen. Click in the Name field, type the variable **continentsVisited**, and press Return. This assigns the name **continentsVisited** to that checkbox. Then, click in the Value field, and type **North America**. When the user looking at your Web site selects this particular checkbox, the value "North America" will be assigned to the variable continentsVisited. Follow these same steps for your other six checkboxes, and make sure that you are giving each one a separate value. For example, your next checkbox will have the name "continentsVisited," but the value "South America"; the next will have the name "continentsVisited," but the value "Europe."

Each window in the Inspector contains a Checked box. Checking this box makes that choice the default. If you are offering your readers choices, though, it doesn't make much sense to have one of them already selected.

After you build your checkboxes, switch to Preview mode and test your work. Look closely at how you entered the names, though, to make sure that you spelled the name exactly the same for each. With the radio buttons, it was easy to determine if you named them correctly, because if you didn't, selecting one would turn off another. With checkboxes, however, it's not as easy to tell if you've named them incorrectly because you should be able to click as many as you like.

Passwords

You can build a Password field into your document. Return to the Password field you created and select the field. In the Attributes Inspector, name this field **secret** and, as always, press Return when you've finished.

Figure 3.12
The Password field of the Attributes Inspector.

Go back to the document window and switch to Preview mode. Click in the Password field you just created and type a few characters. The text should look like Figure 3.13.

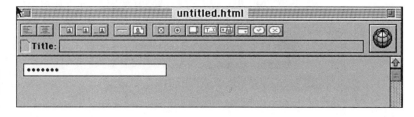

Figure 3.13
Password as it appears on page.

The Password field works identically to the standard text field, but rather than showing the letters that are being input, it just displays dots. This protects your user from only one thing: someone looking over his shoulder. PageMill does not do any type of encryption to the data that is entered into the field. All it does is keep the text from appearing on the monitor of the person browsing your page.

Submit and Reset Buttons

You can include two more buttons in your document. One is optional, the other is absolutely necessary.

The optional button is the Reset button. The job of the Reset button is to clear all the entries in the form. This is helpful if you have a particularly long form. Fortunately, Reset buttons don't have to be named. You just insert one and you're set. To do so, click the last button on the far right of the button bar.

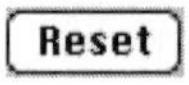

Figure 3.14
Reset button.

Reset

Another button, and the one that is absolutely necessary, is the Submit button. Click the second button to the left on the button bar. A button should appear that looks like the one in Figure 3.15.

Figure 3.15
Submit button.

Submit

The Submit button takes all of the data that your readers entered (along with the individual variable names), packages it, and sends it to your server.

The big question now is, how does the document know where to send the information? This brings us to the next major topic: capturing data.

Retrieving Form Data

Web server software sits on a computer and waits patiently for file requests. It can do a few things with those requests, and a couple things with the files, but essentially its life follows this cycle: A request comes in, and the Web server checks its hard drive to see if it has that particular file. If it does, it ships the file. If it doesn't, it apologizes.

So what happens when your user sends his name, email address, and a list of continents that he has visited instead of a file request? What happens is a CGI.

CGIs

or Common Gateway Interfaces, are small applications that work in conjunction with the Web server to handle some of the things that it can't do alone (like process data from a form).

CGIs are written in a programming language such as C++ or AppleScript (on the Macintosh). If you're a programmer, you might want to look into building a CGI yourself—it isn't difficult. If you're not a programmer, several CGIs already have been built and are available on the Internet as shareware and freeware. CGIs can take the data that has been entered into a form, for example, and place it into a text file, create a new record with it in a database, or put it into an email message and send it to someone.

If you're going to create a form that asks your reader for information, you need a CGI to do something with that form. Point your Web browser to Maxum Development's Web site (`http://www.maxum.com`), and download a copy of NetForms. NetForms is an application that sits on your server, takes the data that is sent to it from a form, and dumps it into a text file or an email message. If you'd like to have the form information posted to a FileMaker Pro database, point your Web browser to Russell Owen's home page (`http://rowen.astro.washington.edu/`) and download the ROFM CGI. If you want to write your own, go to Jon Wiederspan's Extending WebSTAR site (`http://www.uwtc.washington.edu/Computing/WWW/Lessons/START_HERE.html`) where you will find an excellent tutorial on building CGIs that will help you get started.

Manipulating Images

The last task that you will tackle with the Attributes Inspector is manipulating images. Open a new page in PageMill and insert the boots.gif image located in the Images folder of the EarthandWare Tutorial. If you have not already placed an image into a PageMill document, refer to Chapter 2 and see how it is done. Single-click your image to select it. Now click the third button in the Inspector (the same one that you used when you defined variables earlier). Your screen will look like Figure 3.16.

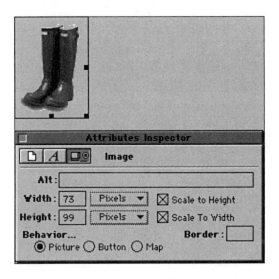

Figure 3.16
Image mode of the Attributes Inspector.

The first box, Alt, is a hold-over from HTML. Alt enables you to provide a contingency plan if your image does not load, which happens surprisingly often, especially if your image takes a long time to transfer. (We'll look at some ways to reduce the size of your image in the next chapter.) Type **This should have been a picture** in the Alt box (see Figure 3.17). If your image fails to load to a viewer's computer, this text will appear. In the future, enter text that provides the reader with more information about what should have loaded.

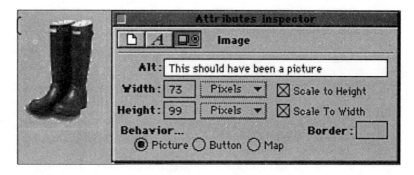

Figure 3.17
The Alt box of the
Image mode.

You saw earlier how you can make images larger or smaller by selecting them and dragging either a corner or a side. That is a fast way of adjusting the size of your image, but if you need to be more exact you should use the Inspector.

Beneath the Alt box you'll see a Width heading and a Height heading. Numbers should appear in the boxes next to the "Width" and "Height" headings. Popup menus let you choose between pixels and percentages. To adjust the size of your image, click inside the box, type a new number, and press Return (one of the scale checkboxes must be unchecked to modify image size).

 Tip

> You can't tab between the boxes or click another one to select it.
> You must press Return first for PageMill to accept the changes
> you have made.

Remember that the size of most Web browser windows is about 480 pixels. You can make images that span more than 480 pixels, but many readers will not be able to see all of the image at once and will need to widen their window to see the entire image. If they have a (gasp!) small monitor, they will have to scroll to see everything.

If you decide to adjust your image based on percent, understand that you are adjusting the width and height independently. This means that if you enter 50% for the height, and your image is currently 2 inches high and 4 inches wide, you will get an image that is 1 inch by 4 inches.

When you place an image onto your document, either by drag-and-dropping or by clicking the Insert Image button, it is not necessarily at 100 percent. PageMill reduces the size somewhat. You'll notice this when you click your image and look at its height and width percentages.

You can maintain the original proportions of an image by holding down the Shift key while you drag the corner of the image. With the Attributes Inspector, you gain even more control over resizing your images while keeping the proportions intact.

To keep the image's proportions intact while resizing, choose to constrain proportions based on either height or width. You can choose to do this in either pixels or percentages. Two checkboxes are to the left of the height and width values. Scale to Height is next to the width box, and Scale to Width is next to the height box. For now, click the Scale to Height box.

When you click the box, some adjustment takes place and the number changes. PageMill looks at the height and adjusts the width so that your image stays proportional. If you click Scale to Width, PageMill looks at the width and adjusts the height. Notice that after you click the Scale to Width box, you can't change the height and vice versa. What you're doing with these checkboxes is locking one dimension. That's not to say the dimension can't be changed; it just can't be changed manually. The dimension is adjusted with a PageMill calculation based on how high or wide you want the other dimension.

Did that make sense? Imagine that an image is 200 pixels wide and 300 pixels high. Let's say you want the image to be only 150 pixels wide. Enter 150 in the width box, and the image changes, giving you a squeezed look. To get rid of the squeeze, adjust the height proportionally. In Figures 3.18 and 3.19, you see two versions of the same image. The first was resized proportionally; the second wasn't. The squeezed effect is what you're trying to avoid.

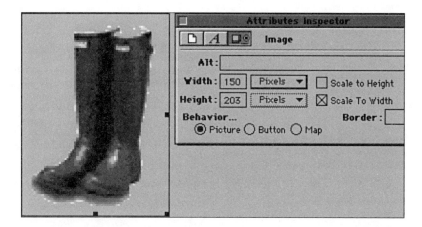

Figure 3.18
An image sized
proportionally.

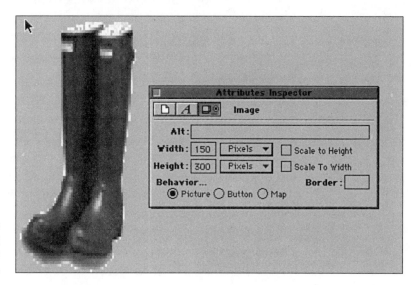

Figure 3.19
The squeezed
appearance of an
image.

You can determine the correct height and width of the image in pixels by doing the calculations in your head (according to the Italian Renaissance artists, your proportions should be around 2:3), eyeballing it until it looks right, or checking the Scale to Width box. If you check Scale to Width, PageMill will consider the width of the image (in this case, 150), and adjust the height to eliminate the squeeze and make your image proportional.

Image Borders

Whenever you place an image into a PageMill document, a border is created. The border is measured in pixels, and you can make it thicker or thinner by adjusting its number of pixels. Chances are, unless you opened the Attributes Inspector, you would never know this because the default border is 0 pixels.

Note

A pixel is one dot on your computer screen.

The border is controlled with the border box in the same window as the image size controls. The thickest you can make the border is 50 pixels. Select your image, and enter 5 in the box at the lower left in the Attributes Inspector. You should see a solid black border around your image.

Why would you ever want to do this? For a few reasons, all having to do with making the image a separate element in your document. If, for example, you make the background of the image transparent to keep the file small (and speed transfer time over the Web), but want the image to be a separate visual element from the rest of the page you can create a border around it. Or, if you left the image's background intact, but changed the background color to something that matches it (for example, if your image has a blue background, and you changed your background color to blue), a border can help distinguish the image.

A set of radio buttons at the bottom of Attributes Inspector's Image mode enables you to control the behavior of the image (by behavior, PageMill means what the image does on the page). PageMill gives you three choices for image behavior:

Figure 3.20
Radio buttons to
control image
behavior.

■ Picture. This simply means that you want this to be an in-line image to be displayed by the browser. This is the default.

■ Button. When you were fooling around with creating links in the previous chapter, did you try to drop a link onto an image? Did you even know that an image could be a link?

In the Edit mode, select the image that you have been working with and choose Button for this image's behavior. A thin blue line appears around the image denoting that it is a link (if you already put a border around the image, it will turn blue), and the Alt box changes to a Name box. Type a URL in the Name box that will be activated when the viewer clicks the image and press Return.

Now, here's something interesting. Go to the border box, enter 0, and press Return. The border disappears. You now have a link that isn't noted in any way. Right about now, that why-would-I-do-this feeling is probably washing over you. Again, this is a design decision that you have to make. If it's obvious that the user is supposed to click the image (say, for example, that it's an image of a button with "click here" on it), having a blue border might be distracting and redundant.

Note

Although you can have a link that isn't noted in any way, if a reader's browser does something special when she moves her mouse over a link—for example, it changes from a pointer to a hand—that still happens.

■ Clickable imagemap. The last option is to turn your image into clickable imagemap. This enables a reader to click different sections of the image and activate links to different URLs. To create a clickable imagemap, select Map, and read the next chapter of this book in great detail. It explains the tools that PageMill provides to create the hot spots on your image.

Text Mode

The last set of features available in the Attributes Inspector is used for general control of the text in your document. Most of the tasks here can be accomplished by using the pull-down menus in PageMill, but you should open the Attributes Inspector and leave it open. The Attributes Inspector provides a quick and easy way to do things. Let's see how this works.

First, open a new page and type a few lines. Be sure to type a few different lines. Highlight the first line of text and click the middle button in the Attributes Inspector (the one with the letter "A" on it). This is the same window where you pointed to the CGI when you built the form. Directly below where you entered the URL for the CGI, you should see a popup menu for aligning the text. Your choices are Left and Center. Although the default option is left aligned, you can center align the text. You cannot, however, right align the text in the current version of PageMill. In addition, PageMill won't let you *justify* (right and left align, or aligned on both sides of the page) text either. The Web does not support justified text.

Justified Text

The rest of the checkboxes in this window of the Attributes Inspector are relatively straightforward. Essentially, you need to highlight the text you want to manipulate and click the corresponding box. Type the text first, and then make your changes to the style. Following are the available styles:

- Plain

- Bold

- Italic

- Teletype

- Strong

- Emphasis

- Citation

- Sample

- Keyboard

- Code

- Variable

Styles can also be combined.

Plain

Choosing Plain is the default style, as defined by the reader in the Preferences file of his or her browser. This is usually a proportional font. This means that letters are kerned, or pushed together, on the screen.

Bold

Choosing Bold sets your text in the bold version of the font used with plain text.

Italic

Choosing Italic sets your text in the italics version of the font used with plain text.

Teletype

Choosing Teletype sets the text in a monospaced font (also defined by the user in the preferences of their browser). Monospaced fonts give the exact same amount of space for each character and don't try to conserve space between letters.

Strong

The Strong attribute is used to make text stand out. For most browsers, text that has the Strong attribute is displayed in bold.

Emphasis

The Emphasis attribute is similar to Strong, except that text with the Emphasis attribute is displayed in italics.

Citation

The Citation attribute is used when you are quoting (or citing) text from another source. Most browsers show text with the Citation attribute in italics.

Other HTML Attributes

The following attributes are an integral part of the original use of HTML: a way to display technical and scientific papers. Most of the following codes are not used outside of academic circles, but PageMill supports them because they are established HTML attributes.

Sample

The Sample attribute is used to display a series of characters taken as a sample from another source. Most browsers display text with the Sample attribute in a monospaced font.

Keyboard

The Keyboard attribute is used to display text meant to be typed. Text with the Keyboards attribute is usually displayed in a monospaced font.

Code

The Code attribute is meant for displaying portions of computer programming code. Text with the Code attribute is usually displayed in a monospaced font.

Variable

The Variable attribute is meant for displaying a variable name within a block of computer programming code. Text with the Variable attribute is usually displayed in italics.

Raw HTML

Raw HTML is unique to PageMill. If you are an HTML writer, you might experience some frustration with PageMill. PageMill is not equipped to handle several things, such as tables, and you are probably accustomed to the high level of control you have when you type HTML directly.

If you really need to type HTML, PageMill enables you to do so and designate it as Raw HTML. When you save your work, PageMill will take everything that you have designated as HTML and include it in the final output, precisely as you typed it.

A Format popup menu also is available in this window. This menu includes all the options that you will find in the Format pull-down menu. This popup puts all the options in one place and makes it easier for you to choose them. If you don't remember what each one does, refer back to Chapter 2 for a complete overview.

Building a Web Page with the Attributes Inspector

In this exercise, you'll build a page using the Attributes Inspector. You will see how to place and control almost all of the elements of images using the Attributes Inspector.

1 Open a new page.

If you don't have it already open, launch PageMill by double-clicking its icon on your hard drive. When you have PageMill open, create a new document by either choosing New Page from the File menu or by typing ⌘-N.

2 Open the Attributes Inspector.

This should be the first step whenever you start a new PageMill document. Open the Attributes Inspector by either selecting "Show Attributes Inspector" from the Window menu or by typing ⌘-;.

The first element to bring in is a background pattern. Drag a GIF file from the Macintosh Finder directly onto the Attributes Inspector.

Figure 3.21
Setting a background image with the Attributes Inspector.

3 Find the EarthandWare Tutorial folder and open the Images folder. Click the icon for `paper1.gif` and drag it to the box in the Attributes Inspector marked backgrd image.

Let's also change the color of the text and the color of any hypertext links. Do this by changing the Text and the Link attributes in the Page mode in the Attributes Inspector.

4 In the Attributes Inspector, find the popup menu next to the Text Attribute and choose Custom. When you are presented with the color wheel, adjust the Lightness (located in the bottom of the window) to 25%. You can do this by either moving the slider with the pointer, typing **25** in the text box for Lightness, or by increasing the lightness with the arrow buttons next to the box. Move the cross-hairs up and to the left inside the circle, at what would be 11:00 if this were a clock face. You should get a dark green. Click OK.

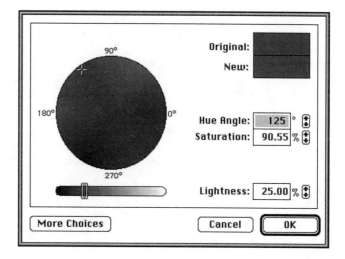

Figure 3.22
Custom color for text.

5 Type **Bob's Boot Emporium Order Form** at the top of the page. Press Return once to go down a line. To make this the largest heading, centered, select the text you typed and click center button in the Attributes Inspector to switch to Text mode. On the left, find the Alignment popup and choose Center. Next to it, in the format popup menu, choose Largest Heading.

You can also make this italics by selecting the Italics checkbox in the first column of the Attributes Inspector.

Now bring in an image to enhance this page.

6 In the Images folder, find the `boots.gif` image. Drag it onto the page below the words (if you pressed Return after you typed the words, you will be able to put the image below the words. If you didn't press Return, PageMill will only be able to place the image next to the words). If you adjusted your text color correctly, the words above the image should match the color of the boots pretty closely.

While the image is still selected, center the boots with the align popup on the Attributes Inspector. Switch to the Image mode of the Attributes Inspector by selecting the third button.

7 This image needs some text that will be shown if it doesn't load correctly. In the Alt box at the top of the Attributes Inspector, type **Boots** and press Return.

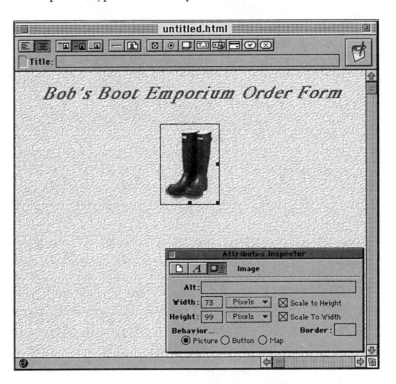

Figure 3.23
Text and Image

Now, you can resize this image, be sure to keep the proportions intact (to avoid a stretched or squeezed effect).

8 In the Image mode of the Attributes Inspector, unclick the Scale to Height checkbox. You can now change the number of pixels high the image is. Change this to 100 and press Return.

Put a border around an image to visually separate this image from the rest of the screen.

9 Type **5** in the box marked Border. This will put a green border five pixels wide around the image of the boots. Your page should now look like this:

Figure 3.24
Image borders.

Create a form that will be used to order boots, you need to start with the tool bar at the top of the main window of PageMill. The form requires four different types of inputs: text fields, popup menus, checkboxes, and radio buttons.

10 Create two text fields with the Insert Text Field button in the PageMill tool bar at the top of the window. Create labels entitled **Name** and **Phone Number** (see Figure 3.25).

Figure 3.25
Text fields.

Create a popup by clicking the Insert popup button. Delete the contents of the popup menu and replace them with **cowboy**, **rain**, **hiking**, and **work**. Label this popup menu **What type of boots would you like to order?** (see Figure 3.26).

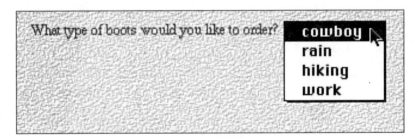

Figure 3.26
Popup menu.

Creating a radio button group.

11 Create one radio button by selecting the Insert Radio Button button at the top of the PageMill window. Select that radio button with the mouse. Option-drag that button to the right

and release the mouse button. Do this five times. Label the radio buttons with the shoe sizes: **10**, **11**, **12**, and **13**. Label the whole group **What size would you like to order?** (see Figure 3.27).

Figure 3.27
Radio buttons.

Use the same procedure to create a checkbox group.

12 Create a checkbox by selecting the Insert Checkbox button from the top of the PageMill window. Select that checkbox and Option-drag it to the left. Do this four times. Label the checkboxes with the following options: **an order verification**, **a catalog**, **a Christmas card**, and **free shoelaces**. Label the whole group **Would you like to receive:**.

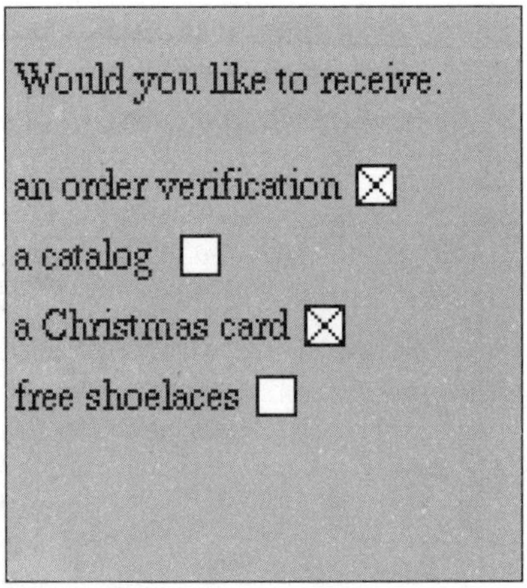

Figure 3.28
Checkboxes in a
form.

Finish the form with the crucial buttons: Submit and Reset.

13 Create a button that will submit this form by selecting the Insert Submit Button button from the top of the PageMill window. Create a reset button by selecting Insert Reset Button (refer to Figures 3.14 and 3.15).

In order to make sure this form works, assign variable names to each one of the input fields.

14 Select the first text field (labeled Name). In the Attributes Inspector, choose Forms mode (button on the far left). Name this field **firstName** in the Name field (be sure to press Return after you change the name of the field). Change the size of the field to 40, and restrict the maximum number of characters that can be put into this field to 50 (see Figure 3.29). Do the same for the phone number field, but name it **phone**. Lengthen the field to 32 characters (so that it lines up with the field above it) and restrict the maximum number of characters that can be input into this field to 50.

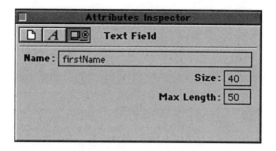

Figure 3.29
Adjusting the size
of the text field.

Naming the popup menu.

15 Select the popup menu and click the third button in the Attributes Inspector. Name this menu **typeBoots,** leave the Items Visible box empty, and the Allow Multiple Selections unchecked. This will create a popup menu where only one item is visible until the menu is selected, and then the user can choose only one item.

To change the name of the radio button and checkbox groups, you need to make sure that each one has the same name, but a different value.

16 Select the first radio button in the radio button group. In the Forms mode of the Attributes Inspector, change the name to **size**, and the value to **10**. Do the same for each of your radio buttons, making sure each has the name **size** and a different value (the values should match the sizes: **11**, **12**, and **13**).

17 Select the first checkbox in the checkbox group you created. In the Forms mode of the Attributes Inspector, change the name to **receive** and the value to **verification**. Do the same for each of the checkboxes, making sure that each has the name **receive** and a different value (these values should match what you have as the options that readers can select: **catalog**, **Christmas card**, and **free shoelaces**).

The last thing the form needs is the location of the CGI that will actually handle the data that the viewers will enter into these fields.

18 In the Attributes Inspector, switch to Page mode by clicking the button on the left (with the icon of the page on it). In the box marked Action, type **test.acgi**, which is the CGI that you want to have this data sent to when the Submit button is pressed. Press Return after you have typed in the CGI name so PageMill will accept the data. The popup next to the Action box must also be on Post.

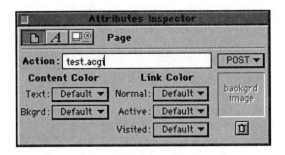

Figure 3.30
Assigning the CGI.

Remember, PageMill will assume that this CGI exists in the folder that you have designated as your local root directory. When you press Return, it will provide the path to that folder in the Action box.

Summary

The Attributes Inspector is the main control panel of PageMill. It is where you control most of the aspects of your document. Using the Attributes Inspector, you can control both the foreground (all the text, including links) and the background colors of your page. You can also place images into the background of the page.

The Attributes Inspector is also used to control the technical details of fill-in forms, including the naming of fields, the method that the server will use to process the data, and the location of the CGI that will actually handle the data.

The Attributes Inspector enables you to manipulate images and control their behavior (to make them into either simply an in-line image, a button that can link to another page or a clickable map). With the Attributes Inspector, an image's border can be added or removed, and the image can be resized while retaining its proportions.

Text attributes are also controlled by the Attributes Inspector. Also, PageMill enables you to include text as Raw HTML.

In the next chapter, you'll learn more about using the image view. You'll learn quick ways to optimize images so that they can be more easily transferred over the Web, and also how to create clickable imagemaps—images with hot spots that will transport your reader to new pages and links.

Chapter 4

Imagemaps and the Image View

PageMill helps you create one of the coolest ways to navigate Web sites: clickable imagemaps. Just as with the fill-in forms created in Chapters 2 and 3, part of creating imagemaps is accomplished by authoring and can be done entirely with PageMill, and part is accomplished by serving, which needs to be done with a CGI on your Web server. PageMill greatly facilitates the authoring of imagemaps with the image view.

This chapter begins by describing the functions of the image view. The remainder of the chapter will teach you how to create your own imagemaps with PageMill.

The Image View

The window in Figure 4.1 is the image view. Inside this window you can control several aspects of the image, including the hot spots that will take the reader to another page when clicked. The only aspect of the image that the image view can't control is its physical size.

Open a new document in PageMill. Drag the image `star.gif` from *The Adobe PageMill Handbook* CD into the new document. Double-click the star to open it in image view.

For a review of how to bring images into your PageMill document, refer to Chapter 2.

 Tip

For a review of how to resize an image, refer to the Attributes Inspector section in Chapter 3.

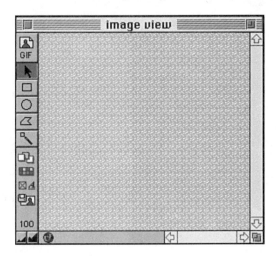

Figure 4.1
The image view
window.

Before you begin creating the map, let's take a look at what you can do with the image view.

Image View Options

In the top left corner of the image view, there is an Image icon with the word GIF under it. GIF is one of the two image formats that can be served over the Web (JPEG is the other). That icon works similarly to how the Image icon worked in the main PageMill window in Edit mode. The icon represents the image, and you can drag-and-drop it onto pages other than the one you are currently working on or onto other elements (images or text) on the page.

Being able to drag-and-drop the Image icon lets you do two things. The first is copy and paste the image into other pages. You can try this now by opening a new page, clicking the Image icon and dragging it onto the new page. It should appear on the new page, as if you copied and pasted it there. Close the second window.

Linking Images and Size Considerations

The Image icon also enables you to create links to external images. Before you ask, here's why you would want a link to an external image: images are big. They take up a lot of space on your hard drive, take a long time to transfer, and, on the Internet, time is definitely money. If you have a large image that takes up a lot of pixels or uses several colors, the file is going to take a great deal of memory and a long time to transfer. Although you might have spent hours making sure that every detail of your hamster Joey's image is absolutely perfect, there is probably a pretty good chance that the user does not want to spend his $4.95 an hour access time downloading it. If you place the image in the document, you don't give the user a choice; when they load your page, they get the picture of Joey.

A better solution, and one that is more user friendly, is to give users the *option* of looking at the 120KB image of Joey. For example, type a line that says, "Here's a 120K picture of my lovely hamster Joey." and make it a link to the image. If someone wants to see it, they can click the link. If not, you haven't wasted their time.

Let's try this in PageMill. You'll create a link to the star.gif image (located in the Images folder on the CD-ROM). If you don't have the image available from the previous example open the image in PageMill with the Open menu option from the File menu (or type ⌘-O). In the Open dialog box, find star.gif and double-click it to open it. The image view will open with the image inside it.

Now, create a new page (by choosing New Page from the File menu, or by typing ⌘-N). In the new page, type **Here's a picture of a star** and use the pointer to highlight the text. Go back to the image view and grab the icon at the top left corner of the window. Without letting go of the mouse button, drag the icon over to the highlighted text in the main PageMill window and release the mouse button.

A link has now been created from this text to the image. You can switch over to Preview mode in PageMill and try this out, if you want. Clicking the text will switch you over to the image view window with the picture of the boots. Over the Web, this image will be displayed in the window of the reader's Web Browser.

Helper Applications

If you surf the Web, you know that there isn't really just one application that you use. The browser software (such as Netscape or Mosaic) is your chief tool for clicking through the Web and reading pages, but the Web is a multimedia environment, complete with sounds, images, and movies. In general, there are way more types of data on the Web than Web browser software can display. One example of this is JPEG images. Currently, only the Netscape Navigator can display JPEG images inside its main window. Other browsers use what is called a helper application to display JPEG images. On the Macintosh, the helper application to view JPEG images is called JPEG View. If the reader of your page is using Mosaic, and comes across a JPEG image, that image is handed off to JPEG View, which displays it in a separate window.

Interlacing Images

In the column of buttons on the left side of the image view is an icon that looks like a floppy disk in front of a person. Single-click this icon and a series of horizontal bars appear across it. This interlaces the image. *Interlaced* is a type of GIF image. When you have interlaced GIFs on your Web page, the browser displays a very low-resolution version of the image first, and then passes over it a few times refining the detail until the reader sees the finished product.

Figure 4.2
The initial displayed view of an interlaced image.

You should interlace all your GIF images. Interlaced GIFs give the reader a preview of what is to come, and show that the server is active and in the process of sending the image. User patience with slow-loading graphics is notorious. Interlaced GIFs are an excellent way to get the reader's attention and hold it during the sometimes arduous process of image loading. Some browsers have the added benefit of loading text before the image's detail is refined enabling the reader to view text while waiting for the image to appear.

Transparent Images

In the middle of the tool bar in the image view window is a button marked with a magic wand icon. The magic wand is used to turn the background of any GIF image transparent. Turning backgrounds transparent is a pretty important step to take for images that are going to be displayed over the Web for two big reasons: the images will look better and load quicker.

First, an explanation of what is meant by making the background transparent. All GIF images are saved with a background, which is usually white. If you have a non-rectangular image, it will be displayed on your Web page with a white rectangle around it. Because the default background on most Web browsers is gray, this will make your image look out of place on the page (see Figure 4.3).

When you make the background transparent, the color of the Web browser's window will show (see Figure 4.4). The image looks more integrated into the page. This will also hold true if you change the background of your page (see Chapter 3 for details on how to change the background of the window).

The image loads faster when the background is transparent. The reason for this is simple: removing the background makes the file size of the image smaller. The image in Figure 4.3 takes 22K of disk space. The image in Figure 4.4—which is exactly the same image, but with the transparent background—takes up 11K. As mentioned earlier, the smaller the image file, the faster it will load. Making an image's background transparent is a quick way to decrease the file size of your images.

Drag the star.gif file into the Content Area of PageMill. Return to the image view of the star.gif file and select the magic wand tool. Click the white background and your image becomes transparent. You'll need to save the image for it to become transparent on your page.

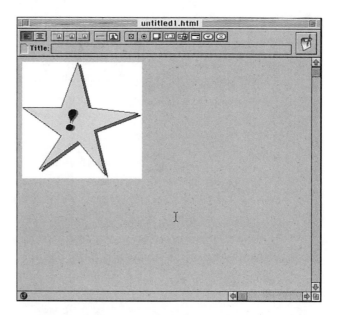

Figure 4.3
An image with a white background.

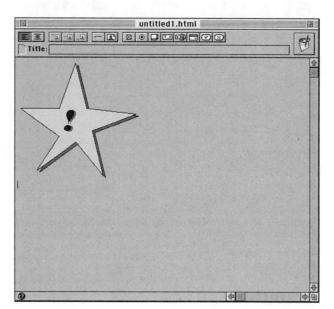

Figure 4.4
An image with a transparent background.

Making an image transparent reduces the memory size of your image. A white background makes the image large and time-consuming to transfer. Removing the white background decreases the amount of time your page takes to load, and makes it look better. How often does that happen?

Zoom Tools

The last set of tools in the image view is the zoom tools. In the lower left corner of the image view window are two landscape icons. The one on the right zooms in to the image; the one on the left zooms out. This doesn't change the size or appearance of the image in your document, just your view of it. You can enlarge your view of the image 800 percent, and reduce your view to 12 percent.

What is an Imagemap?

Have you ever visited a Web site that had a graphic with hot spots that, depending on what part of the graphic you clicked, took you to different parts of the Web site? These are called *imagemaps*. For an example of an imagemap, go to Apple Computer's Web site at `http://www.apple.com`.

Imagemaps are different from the buttons you created with the Attributes Inspector in Chapter 3. On a button, the URL is attached to the entire image, and you are always taken to the same URL no matter where you click the image.

Imagemaps are different, in that you—as the creator of the imagemap—can attach different URLs to different regions of a single image. When the user clicks a particular area of the image, it activates a specific URL.

Note

Remember, URLs can point to anything on the Internet, including pages on your own Web site or another Web site entirely.

How Do Imagemaps Work?

For imagemaps to work, you need a CGI (Common Gateway Interface). Remember, CGIs are the small applications that work in conjunction with the Web server software to extend the functionality of your Web site. In the case of imagemaps, the CGI receives a set of coordinates that the user clicked (like 14, 160, meaning 14 pixels over from the upper left corner of the image and 160 pixels down), converts them to a URL, and passes the URL back to the server. The coordinates are determined based on where you click the mouse.

Let's say you created the image in Figure 4.5 in your graphics application and plan to use it as an imagemap. Open a new document in PageMill. Drag the `image_map.gif` file from the CD into the new document. When you have placed it in the PageMill window, double-click the image, which will open the image view window where you'll assign the regions.

Figure 4.5
A single graphic
image.

To create an imagemap, you need to map out different regions on the image and assign different URLs to each region. In this section, you will highlight the area Document #1 and attach a URL. Then you'll do the same for the area Document #2, but attach a different URL.

Mapping the Regions

Defining a specific region of an imagemap involves determining which pixels belong to a particular area. (The word pixel is a combination of the words picture and element.) Everything displayed on a monitor, from a picture of the Mona Lisa, which you can download from the Louvre Web site (`http://www.paris.org/Musees/Louvre/Treasures/`), to the letters in a word are made up of pixels.

Pixels are the dots that are used to create an image on a computer monitor.

If you know that the image that you plan to use as an imagemap is really just a series of dots arranged in rows and columns, you can imagine that there is a grid that overlays the image where each pixel has a corresponding set of coordinates. Using this imaginary grid, you can refer to individual pixels by their coordinates—the number of pixels across and down the screen. The uppermost left pixel then is 0,0.

Let's say that this image is 450 pixels wide and 200 pixels tall. The extreme lower right pixel, then, is 450, 200. (Coordinates are always given as number of pixels across, number of pixels down.) Figure 4.6 shows the coordinates mapped onto the image. When you did graphing in geometry or algebra class, the number of pixels across was always copied into a variable called x; the number of pixels down was copied into a variable called y (oh no! variables again!). The main difference here from the graphing done in algebra or geometry, is that the coordinate 0,0 is the top left corner. In algebra and geometry 0,0 is the lower left corner.

(0,0)   (450, 0)

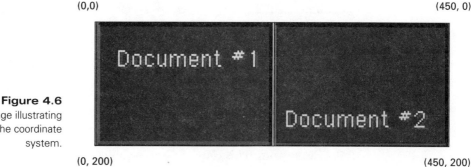

Figure 4.6
Image illustrating
the coordinate
system.

(0, 200)   (450, 200)

URLs are activated when certain pixels in an imagemap are
clicked. In Figure 4.7, the image is shown with the middle line at
pixel 225, 0. The bottom of the line is 225, 200. If the user selects
a pixel to the left of that line (that is, with a value in the x variable
that is less than 225), you want the server to access the URL to
retrieve document #1. If the user clicks a pixel to the right of the
line (with an *x* value that is greater than 225), you want the server
to access the URL to retrieve document #2.

(225, 0)

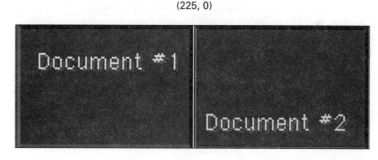

Figure 4.7
The division of the
two areas by the
coordinate system.

(225, 200)

Creating the Imagemap

Imagemaps can be created from any GIF image, but your image
should have some visual clues as to what each one of the regions
does or where they take you. Go back to the image you dropped
onto the page with the two areas—one to document #1, the other

to document #2. First, you need to attach the URL for document #1 to all the pixels left of the dividing line. Return to the image view.

A column of buttons is on the left side of the image view, below the Image icon. Each one is a tool. If you have ever used a drawing program, these should look familiar to you. They are as follows:

- Pointer tool. This is used to move objects around.

- Rectangle tool. This is used to define areas with four right angles.

- Circle tool. This is used to define areas circular objects.

- Polygon tool. This is used to define areas objects with multiple sides, all made of straight lines.

Note

You cannot draw with PageMill. All of your images need to be created in some other application. The `circle`, `rectangle`, and `polygon` tools in the image view are used to map out the regions to which you want to attach URLs.

In the image with which you are working, create a rectangular region to which the URL is attached `http://your_web_site/document_one.html`. Select the Rectangle tool (second one down) and draw a rectangle from the left edge of the image to the dividing line. You just specified a particular group of pixels, all of the ones within the rectangle that you drew. Now you need to attach the URL.

Find the Globe icon at the bottom of the image view. Click to the right of it; a blinking cursor appears. Enter the URL to be attached to this group of pixels. Type **`http://your_web_site/document_one.html`** in the space provided and press Return. This URL now appears inside the rectangle that you drew. If the URL is not there, click the checkbox with the letter A (on the left side of the image view). With this checkbox, you can either have the URL displayed inside the image view or not.

The default color of the URL and the area that you defined is blue, but you can change this with the Color Palette icon (third from the bottom). You don't have many choices. The important thing is to make the URL a color that stands out from the image so that it is easier to see.

Now, do the same for the other side of the dividing line. Create a rectangle that extends from the dividing line to the edge of the image. Type `http://your_web_site/document_two.html` in the space provided next to the Globe icon.

You have created the regions of the imagemap and attached the URLs to them. Now, you need to put this information into a format usable by the CGI (see Chapter 5), which will eventually serve these pages by writing a map file. Don't worry, PageMill does this for you. After all, PageMill is meant to make this process easy, right?

Imagemap Preferences

A step in creating a map file is setting your Map format preference. Go to the Preferences located under the Edit pull-down menu. The second item in the Preferences is Image Preferences. There is a popup menu that asks you what format you want for your map file. Map files are text documents that describe the regions that you defined in your imagemap, as well as the URLs that are attached to them. Map files can be formatted as either NCSA or CERN files. NCSA is the National Center for Supercomputing Applications. CERN is a French abbreviation for the European Particle Physics Lab. Both organizations are largely responsible for the standards of the World Wide Web, and both have a format for creating imagemaps. Find out which method your server is using and create a map file that is compatible with it. If you are serving your imagemap from a Macintosh and using the `imagemap.acgi` that is provided on the CD, choose NCSA. Click to save and the Preferences.

Close the image view. A dialog box appears asking if you want to save the changes to your image. Choose Save. In PageMill's main window, you won't see the rectangles or the URLs you placed on the image. Remember, you are not actually doing anything to the image when you create an imagemap. All you are doing is creating a map file, which will be used by the CGI to transform the coordinates into a URL which it will send back to the server.

Accessing the Imagemap File

Map files are stored in the Images folder on your hard drive. For now, quit PageMill and open the Images folder on your hard drive. You should see the icon for the image that you used as an imagemap, as well as a SimpleText document with the file extension .map. Open the map file. If you chose NCSA format, it should look something like this:

```
rect        http://your_web_site/document_two.html 144,0
290,155 rect

http://your_web_site/document_one.html 0,0 144,154
```

This is your map file. If your map file does not look exactly like this, don't worry. Your coordinates will, of course, be different and sometimes PageMill puts all the information on a single line. These lines are instructions that eventually will be picked up by the CGI and used to determine what to do when it receives a set of coordinates (you'll see how to set this up on your server next).

Each line of the map file consists of three sections. The first section tells you what type of region the map file is referring (in this case, "rect" is short for rectangle). The next section is the URL, and the last section holds the coordinates that are attached to this URL. In this case, only two sets of coordinates are needed: the upper left corner and the lower right corner. Because this is a rectangle, known from the first bit of information, only two sets of coordinates are needed to draw the complete region.

How an Imagemap Works

Warning! This section is pretty techno-Web geeky. If you're not interested, skip ahead and leave the rest of us to our propeller hats. Your Webmaster should understand this information. It's not required knowledge if you're serving documents on a server someone else is managing.

As you recall, the primary function of server software is receiving requests and sending files. All other duties are delegated to the CGIs on the server computer. When a user clicks a pixel inside an imagemap, the browser software sends the coordinates of the mouse click to the server. Those mouse click coordinates then get delegated to a CGI that handles imagemaps.

The imagemap CGI contains rules. Rules are the basis of all computer applications, in the form of if…then statements. The application receives some information and passes that information through its if…then statements. It then performs actions based on the results.

 Note

An if…then statement is a statement that says, if a certain condition exists (like a number being within a certain range), then perform an action. If…then statements are also called *conditionals*.

The imagemap CGI has a series of if…then statements that help it decide which file is being requested by the user. You can imagine that, inside of the CGI, there are some rules that look like this:

If *x* is greater than 144 and less than 290,

and if *y* is greater then 0 and less than 155,

then tell the Web server to send document two.html to the user.

If *x* is greater than 0 and less than 144,

and *y* is greater than 0 and less than 154,

then tell the Web server to send document_one.html to the user.

So, let's say the user clicks coordinates 18, 95 and they are sent to the CGI. The CGI receives this as *x*=18&*y*=95. The CGI then passes these coordinates through the rules described above, and comes to the conclusion that it needs to tell the server to send out document_one.html.

The way the CGI and Web server software communicate is pretty complex, and is not within the scope of this book. For our purposes, let's just say that they are able to exchange information freely and with relative ease. If you want to find out how it is accomplished on the Macintosh with WebSTAR server software, you can start at `http://www.biap.com` and follow links to the Datapig.

Creating the If...Then statements

By using the image view tools and outputting the map file, you have already defined the regions of your imagemap. Now you need to place this file somewhere that the imagemap CGI can find and use it. The process that we'll describe here is how to do this with a Macintosh server and the `imagemap.acgi` that is provided on *The PageMill Handbook* CD.

If you are using a computer other than a Macintosh to serve your Web pages, you won't be able to use the `imagemap.acgi` that is described here. Some servers on other platforms don't need an external application to serve imagemaps. For example, NCSA HTTPd, which runs under Unix, is able to understand the information in the map file and serve files based on that information all by itself.

On the Macintosh, Web server software can serve files that are either in the same folder as the server software, or in a subfolder (there are, however, some ways to get around this using aliases). Locate the Utilities folder on *The PageMill Handbook* CD. Open the folder called `imagemap.acgi.` and find the application `imagemap.acgi` and the file imagemap config. Drag both of these files to the folder on your Web server's hard drive containing the server software.

If you have not done so already, create an imagemap. When your imagemap is complete, and you have closed the image view, find the map file that was created. Place the map file in the same folder as the imagemap.acgi on your server, and then (this is important for the example) rename the map file `test.gif.map`.

 Note

The map file is located in the Images folder on the top level of your hard drive.

The imagemap.acgi is able to read this map file and execute the rules that you have set. When imagemap.acgi is launched, it finds your map file and reads information it contains. You need to tell imagemap.acgi what map file to read in. You do this in the config file (which should be in the same folder as the CGI). Open the imagemap config file. It is a text document, so you should be able to open it with SimpleText or TeachText.

The config file contains a number of ⌘s to the server. At the very bottom of the config file, there is a line that looks like this:

```
nonmap : :nonmap.gif.map
```

This is how you point to a map file for the CGI. The imagemap.acgi can serve any number of imagemaps, as long as it knows what set of instructions (or map file) to use for each imagemap. The CGI associates map files with specific keywords that work as triggers. In this case, "nonmap" is a trigger word for a map file named `nonmap.gif.map`.

If this is your first time doing this, don't worry about that last paragraph being really confusing. What we're telling you is that you need to pick a trigger word to associate with the imagemap you have created. The CGI will receive the trigger word as a part of the URL and use the appropriate set of instructions to determine what file to tell the server to send out. For now, add this line to the bottom of the config file (make sure that you put this in exactly as it is here, spaces and all).

```
test : :test.gif.map
```

This instruction tells the CGI to use the `test.gif.map` map file when it receives the "test" trigger word. You did name that map file test.gif.map, right? Otherwise, this example won't work.

Now, you need to send the right trigger word to our CGI. This is back to authoring, so go to PageMill and open the document that contains the imagemap. Single-click the imagemap and open the Attributes Inspector. Click the far left button to get the attributes for the image. At the bottom of the Attributes Inspector, you have three choices regarding the behavior of the image. Choose the far left Map button. This is one of those can't-not-do, won't-work-if-you-forget steps. Clicking this button puts a command into the final output file that tells the browser software to treat this image as a map.

Next, click the middle button, the one with the italic letter *A* on it. This mode enables you to adjust the attributes of the text on your page. The part, however, that we're concerned with is the Location box. This is where you can turn an element into a hypertext link.

An imagemap is really just a bunch of links, all of which are controlled by one CGI on your server. Therefore, you need to link this imagemap to the application—the CGI. Also, we have to tell the CGI from which imagemap this mouse click originated. To accomplish this we need to hard-code the trigger word.

trigger word will tell the imagemap.acgi which map file is needed. The map file will then, in turn, determine which file to tell the server to serve.

Let's do this in two parts. The first part, linking to the CGI, is easy. Before you build the link, though, make sure that `imagemap.acgi`, the imagemap config file, and the map file that you created with the rules for this particular map are all in the same folder called imagemaps. Then type the following into the Location box (located at the top of the Attributes Inspector Window): **imagemaps/imagemap.acgi**. I know you've gotten into the excellent habit of pressing Return after everything you do in PageMill, but suppress that urge for a minute. You still need to do the second part of the URL.

The second part is hard-coding the trigger word that will tell the CGI which map file to use for this particular imagemap. *Hard-coding* means putting the trigger word in a place that can't be changed by the user. It is something that is set beforehand as a part of the URL to the CGI. The trigger word is a little extra piece of information passed to the CGI by making it a part of the URL that calls the CGI. In order for us to pass information to the CGI, the trigger word must be put into the URL in a special way: behind a dollar sign ($). The trigger word for the CGI is "test." Our full URL should look like this:

```
imagemaps/imagemap.acgi$test
```

This is the complete URL that you type into the Location window in the Attributes Inspector. Press Return. When this imagemap is finally served on a page, and a pixel on the imagemap is finally clicked, the browser will attach the coordinates to the URL behind a question mark (?). What the server finally gets looks like this:

```
imagemaps/imagemap.acgi?180,75$test
```

This is all the information the CGI needs to know to tell the server to send out document_one.html.

More about Defining Clickable Regions

PageMill can create clickable regions in shapes other than simple rectangles. Open a new document in PageMill. From *The PageMill Handbook* CD, drag the image image_map2.gif into the new document. Double-click the image to open the image view as shown in Figure 4.8. You can use the rectangle, circle, and polygon tools to define areas of this image.

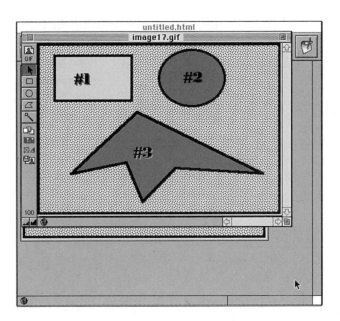

Figure 4.8
An imagemap file showing irregular clickable areas.

Single-click the Circle tool in the image view. You can use this to define circular regions and attach URLs to them the same way you did with the Rectangle tool. Define the region and type the URL in the space next to the Globe icon at the bottom of the image view.

Define a circular area around region #2 as shown in Figure 4.8. Notice you are not drawing ovals with this tool. You cannot define oval regions with PageMill. This is a limitation of PageMill. There is a reason for this: The CGI wants the region defined by a center point and a point on the radius. This is only possible if the region is a perfect circle. When you use the Circle tool to define a region, the point at which you press down on the mouse button is the upper left corner of a square that encloses the circle.

The Polygon tool is used to define regions that have many sides in which all lines are straight. When using the Polygon tool, the first mouse click becomes the first point of your polygon. You then get a line from that point that you can extend in any direction and any length. The next mouse click becomes the second point, giving you a second line that you can extend any direction and any length. Try to define area #3 in Figure 4.8 with the Polygon tool. When you have created the perfect polygon, double-click the mouse. This will draw a line from the last point you made to the first point, closing the polygon. Type the URL into the space at the bottom of the window next to the Globe icon and press Return.

Editing Defined Regions

When you have mapped a few regions on the image, you may need to adjust them. This is no problem, because the image view is object-oriented. Click the Pointer tool (just below the Image icon). You can select objects by simply clicking them. You can drag the region or resize it by clicking one of its corners. You can do this with any of the objects that you have created. Remember, if you have already saved the map file, and then make any changes, you'll need to save again to make sure that your CGI has the correct, updated map file.

Object-oriented vs. Bitmap

Computers have two ways of understanding shapes on the screen. One is called *bitmapped*. The other is called *object-oriented*. Bitmapped means that the computer just knows that there are a bunch of pixels on the screen. Object-oriented means that, if you draw a circle, the computer knows that it is a complete object. With applications that are object-oriented, you can draw an object (an object being and line, dot, polygon, circle, and so on), then select it with the pointer and resize it or move it to a new location. PageMill is object-oriented.

Note

URLs can point to anything on the Internet. Try experimenting with the URLs that you are putting into the Location box. Try linking to other Web sites, email addresses, or FTP sites.

Exercise: Using the Image View

In this exercise, you will control some aspects of an image and create an imagemap with the image view window and the Attributes Inspector.

1 If you don't already have PageMill open, launch it by double-clicking its icon. Create a new page by either typing ⌘-N or by selecting New Page from the File menu.

The image you will be working with is a map of the world. This exercise will make each of the continents a clickable region that will take the reader to a page that describes the continent.

2 On *The PageMill Handbook* CD-ROM, find the Images folder inside the Self-Guided PageMill Tutorial folder. Click the icon for the image11.gif image and drag it onto your new page.

3 Double-click the image of the world that you placed onto your page. This will open up the image view window (see Figure 4.9).

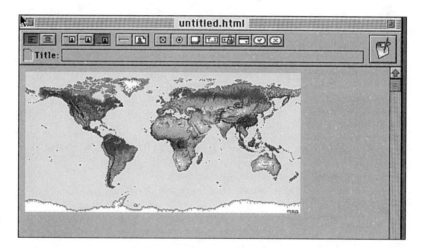

Figure 4.9
Map of the World.

The first thing to do is to take away the background of the image. In this image, all of the oceans are background.

4 In Image View, select the Magic Wand icon. Move the pointer so that you are over any of the light blue portion of the image. Click once, and the blue will turn gray. This means that all light blue portions have been made transparent.

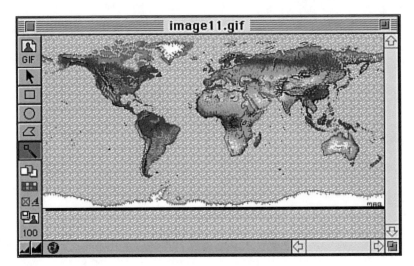

Figure 4.10
Image View.

Now make the image interlaced, so that when it loads it will have that coming-into-focus effect.

5 Almost at the bottom of the image view window is an icon of a person with a floppy disk on it. Click this once so that a series of horizontal lines break up the icon of the person. The image is now interlaced.

Next, you'll create the regions of the image that will be used as hot spots.

6 Make each continent a hot spot. Start with South America. Click the Circle tool and define a circle that encloses all of South America. It will be difficult to get it exact, but remember that PageMill is object-oriented, so you can resize and move the circular region that you have defined. Your map should look like Figure 4.11.

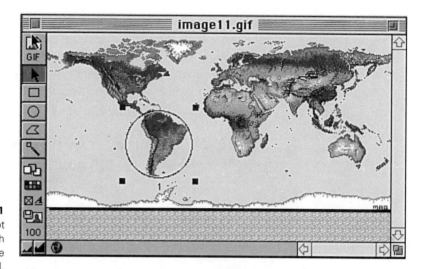

Figure 4.11
Defining the Hot
Spot for South
America with the
circle tool.

Next, define the hot spot for Australia. You can use the Rectangle tool for this, because Australia is somewhat rectangular.

7 Zoom in on the image by clicking once on the zoom-in button (located in the lower left corner of the image view window). Select the Rectangle tool. Position the pointer in the upper left corner of Australia. Press the mouse button, drag the pointer down to the lower left corner of Australia, and release (see Figure 4.12).

Use the Polygon tool for the rest of the continents, because they are irregularly shaped.

8 Stay zoomed-in on the image. Choose the Polygon tool, move the pointer over to the top left corner of Alaska, and click once. Move the pointer down along the edge of Alaska, creating a line down to where the Aleutian Islands begin to spread out. Press the mouse button again, creating another point. Continue doing this, creating lines and points

enclosing the entire North American continent. When you have made it all the way around the East coast of America and Canada, and up and around Greenland and back across the northern end of the continent, double-click the mouse, and a line will automatically be drawn back to the first point you created, making this polygon closed.

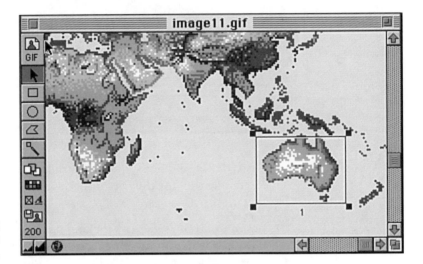

Figure 4.12
Defining Australia with Rectangle tool.

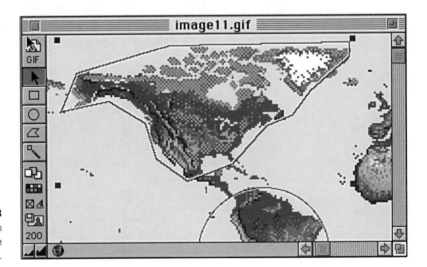

Figure 4.13
Defining North America. with the Polygon tool.

You now have three regions, but need four more.

9 Using the same technique described in Step 8, create hot spots for Europe, Asia, Antarctica, and Africa. When you are done, your map should resemble the one in Figure 4.14.

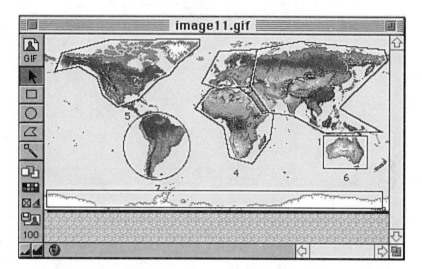

Figure 4.14
The continents.

The next step is to attach the names of the files you want to be served when the reader clicks inside one of these hot spots.

10 Select the Pointer tool (the Arrow icon). Select the region that you defined for North America (when you select the region, squares appear in each of the four corners of the rectangle that bounds the polygon). In the bottom of the image view window, find the Globe icon. With the pointer, click once in the space next to the icon. Type **north_america.html** in this space and press Return (see Figure 4.13). Repeat this process for each of the continents, using the file names: south_america.html, africa.html, europe.html, asia.html, australia.html and antarctica.html.

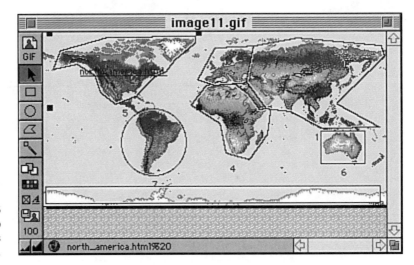

Figure 4.15
Defining Imagemap
with Attributes
Inspector.

Now, write the map file, which will be used either by the server or a CGI to turn a reader's mouse click into a file.

11 Save your work by either typing ⌘-S or by selecting Save from the File menu. In the Images folder on your hard drive, find a text file with the `.map extension`. This is the map file for this imagemap.

This image also needs to be defined as an imagemap with the Attributes Inspector.

12 Close the image view by single-clicking the box in the upper left corner of the window. In the main PageMill window, your image should still be selected. Open the Attributes Inspector by either typing ⌘-; or by selecting Show Attributes Inspector from the Window menu. It should be in Image mode (if not, click the button on the far right). At the bottom of the Attributes Inspector, find the three radio buttons and select Map. Save this entire page as continents.html. Copy the contents of the PageMill Self-Guided Tutorial folder to your hard drive and place them in the same folder as continents.html. So, in one folder, you need: continents.html, the files north_america.html, south_america.html, asia.html, europe.html, antarctica.html, africa.html, and australia.html.

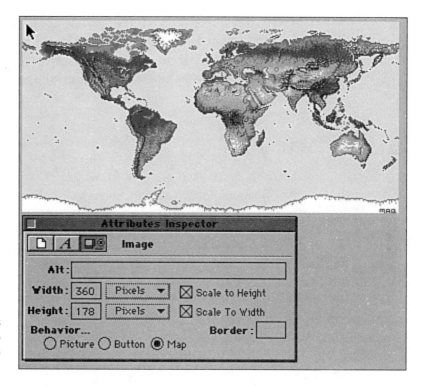

Figure 4.16
Defining Imagemap
with Attributes
Inspector.

You can now test out your imagemap. Switch to Preview mode and click on the various regions that you've defined. Remember that you need a server to have imagemaps really work. If you open this file locally with Netscape or any other browser software, it will not work like it does in PageMill.

If you are going to use the CGI that comes with this book to serve this map from your Macintosh Web server, remember to put **imagemap.acgi** in the Location box of the Attributes Inspector's Text mode. Also, place the page you created with the imagemap and the map file in the same folder as the CGI. Be sure to follow the directions in Chapter 3 for setting the configuration file of the imagemap.acgi so that the CGI knows which map file to use for which imagemap.

If your Web server is on another platform, such as Unix or Windows, or if your server is able to handle imagemaps without needing a CGI, make sure that you put the map file in a place where the server can find it. You can probably find out this information from the person who administers your server.

Summary

This chapter showed you how to use the image view and to turn your images into clickable imagemaps. Imagemaps are a popular way to spruce up your Web pages. Now PageMill can make defining the maps easy.

Chapter 5

Common Gateway Interfaces

You probably have a general understanding of what a CGI is and how it works. In this chapter, you're going to solidify that knowledge and learn about the CGIs that are available on the Internet.

What is a CGI?

A *CGI* is an application that works with a Web server to extend its functionality. CGIs have been written for every computer platform (including Macintosh, Windows, and UNIX) and can be written in almost any programming language. Web servers can pass information to CGIs (see Figure 5.1) as well as receive information from CGIs. CGIs can be launched by the Web server and can interact with applications other than the Web server (see Figure 5.2).

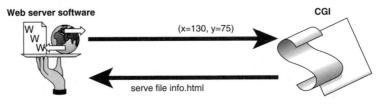

Figure 5.1

Web servers can send information to CGIs, and vice versa.

The Web server gives the CGI some information, which it passes through its set of rules, then sends some information back to the Web server instructing it as to what to do next.

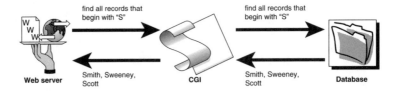

Figure 5.2

CGIs can enable Web servers to interact with other applications.

The CGI can also act as an intermediary between the Web server and another application. The database doesn't know how to communicate with the Web server and vice versa. The CGI takes care of all of the communication.

The two main functions that CGIs perform are data capture and image mapping. Those, however, are not the only functions they perform. CGIs extend the interactivity of your Web site by allowing you to include features such as email, searching, and access counters.

How CGIs Work

CGIs spring into action when they receive a message from the Web server. The message from the Web server launches the CGI application. After the CGI has been launched, it follows its instructions just like an application you would use on your computer.

CGIs are applications written by computer programmers. These applications can have a few simple instructions or a long list of instructions. A simple CGI, for example, is the imagemap you worked through in Chapter 4. A more complex example is writing information from a form on a Web server to a database.

Writing CGIs

When the Web was first developed it was necessary to write your own CGIs. If you could program applications on your computer, the transition to writing CGIs was fairly easy. Essentially, you would include information in your program that enabled your application to communicate with the Web server software. If you weren't a programmer, you either learned the skills necessary to create your applications or just accepted the fact that you could only create HTML pages without cool stuff.

In the early days of the Web, an information provider needed two diverse skill sets to create a Web site: the ability to create good information systems and the ability to write computer code. This, of course, is a bad model. The idea that you needed two very different skill sets was ridiculous. The desire to overturn this model was part of what spurred the creation of PageMill. It also led to a growing community of programmers who began to create CGIs that everyone could use on their Web sites without having to program the applications themselves.

The proliferation of available CGIs is almost at a point where building a Web site is like piecing together a puzzle. You can start with Web pages and add to them with CGIs. This is analogous to using Adobe PageMaker. Most designers know PageMaker extremely well but use plug-ins to extend the functionality of PageMaker. This way, they can add effects to their pieces without knowing the technical details of how the effects are created.

Several applications support plug-ins. Plug-ins are small pieces of software that work within the larger framework and functionality of an application. For example, there are plug-ins for Adobe Photoshop that enable you to create visual effects.

Literally dozens of CGIs are available to use on your Web site. But, there is a chance that you won't find one that does exactly what you want it to do. Or, you might be one of the brave few—a real power user—who wants to get into Web publishing and write your own CGIs.

If you want to write your own CGIs, you need to know a few things first. If you already know how to program an application on your computer, check out the following online resources for writing CGIs:

- Jon Wiederspan's Extending WebSTAR site at `http://www.uwtc.washington.edu/Computing/WWW/Lessons/START_HERE.html`

- Eric Lease Morgan's hypertext book, *Teaching a New Dog Old Tricks* at `http://152.1.24.177/teaching/manuscript/default.html`

These sites will help you understand how to build code that accepts the messages from the Web server and talks back to it.

Both resources focus on AppleScript, which is a good place to start. If you know another language, you should be able to take the concepts discussed here and apply them to that particular language.

If you've never written a computer program before, you need to learn a programming language. If you are using a Macintosh server, you probably should start with AppleScript or Aretha.

Writing CGIs in AppleScript

AppleScript is the scripting language from Apple Computer. It has excellent capabilities as a CGI language and is relatively easy to understand.

If you installed System 7.5, you have AppleScript. AppleScript is easy to use and it can communicate with other applications. AppleScript, however, is not as powerful as some other programming languages (officially, AppleScript is not a programming language, but a scripting language), and it cannot perform some tasks as quickly as languages such as C++. Unfortunately, the documentation that comes with AppleScript is poor. You should refer to two books for more information: *The Tao of AppleScript* and *Danny Goodman's AppleScript* book. Both will get you on your way to writing AppleScripts.

Scripting Additions can be thought of as small applications that perform basic tasks.

As a solution to AppleScript's slowness, and also to help AppleScripters write solid scripts without having to write for mundane or basic tasks, Apple built in support for Scripting Additions. The only difference between a Scripting Addition and an application is that Scripting Additions can't be launched by double-clicking them; they must be launched by an AppleScript.

Writings CGIs in Aretha

Aretha is another language that is starting to be used heavily for creating Macintosh CGIs. Aretha began life as UserLand Frontier, which was the first Macintosh scripting language. Its inventor, Dave Winer, has since released a free version of the language. Aretha is gaining popularity as a CGI language because it is faster than AppleScript. To get a copy of Aretha, go to `http://www.hotwired.com/staff/userland/aretha`. You'll also find documentation and a few sample CGI scripts written in Aretha.

CGIs in Other Languages

AppleScript and Frontier are not the only alternatives for coding CGIs on the Macintosh. We said earlier that you can write a CGI in almost any programming language. Programmers have written CGIs in MacPerl, C++, and even Future Basic.

If you are familiar with any of these languages, you probably can write a CGI in them. Remember, though, that we are strictly talking about writing CGIs for the Macintosh. In general, the CGIs you create will not be cross-platform. Even scripts written in MacPerl, which is based on Perl, a UNIX scripting language, can't be written on a Macintosh and placed on a UNIX box.

Here is a Web site that provides information for writing CGIs in MacPERL: `http://www.biap.com/machttp/howto_perl.html`.

CGIs for Macintosh

Many resources exist on the Web. For a great resource try Jon Wiederspan's list of CGIs at `http://ww.uwtc.washington.edu/Computing/WWW/Mac/CGI.html`. These CGIs should work on any Macintosh Web server.

Note

If you don't have a Macintosh server set up, you can download a free trial version of WebSTAR from StarNine's Web site (http://www.starnine.com).

To use these CGIs, the server must be running. CGIs work closely with the Web server and are dependent upon it to supply information; they won't work without it.

Data Capture CGIs

When you used PageMill to create fill-in forms in Chapter 4, the last step you took was to point to a CGI in the Attributes Inspector. Chapter 4 talked about variables and how they were containers for the data that the viewer was going to input (either into the text areas we created or by choosing one of the radio buttons or checkboxes that we provided). It also talked about how the containers would then be sent to the server to be processed.

Well, imagine that you are now inside the server, and this bundle of variables containing information has just arrived after a viewer clicked on a form's Submit button. What are you going to do with it? You can't just let it go out into cyberspace. That would defeat the purpose of asking for it in the first place. What you need to do is store the information somewhere. You can store the information in the following places:

- Text file
- Database

In this section, you'll look at some of the Macintosh CGIs that are available for collecting data from Web forms.

ROFM CGI

The first CGI that you'll learn about is one that lets you interface your Web site with the database application Claris FileMaker Pro. The CGI that comes from Russell Owens at the University of Washington is free, and you can download the latest version from Russell's Web site at `http://rowen.astro.washington.edu/`.

You do, of course, need to have FileMaker installed (and actually, you need at least version 2.3) to use the CGI. No programming is required, but you do have to do something a little unusual with your Web pages (and, unfortunately, something that you can't do easily with PageMill): create hidden fields.

Do a quick walk through on this. Launch PageMill and create a simple form. Place the cursor somewhere near the top of your page and type the following:

```
<INPUT TYPE="HIDDEN" NAME="_database" VALUE="bb.db">
```

Now, highlight this text with the pointer and open the Attributes Inspector. Click on the Raw HTML checkbox in Text mode. You have just added HTML to your form that will act as an instruction to the CGI.

The CGI takes the data that has been input into the fields and processes them. For most fields, it simply takes what your reader typed and plugs it into a record in the database. But, this particular CGI looks for a few special fields for instructions as to what it should do. The code that you enter here is a message telling the CGI that it should put the information from this form into a database called bb.db.

Unfortunately, this example won't work. One of the requirements of this CGI is that the names of your fields in your Web page match with the names of the fields in your FileMaker database.

So, if you create a field in your Web page called "email" (using the Attributes Inspector to name the field as you did in Chapter 3), you need to create a field in your FileMaker database called "email."

Like many Macintosh CGIs, ROFM is written in AppleScript. The CGI ROFM uses four Scripting Additions: Decode URL, Encode URL, DePlus, and ACME Parse Args. Don't worry about what each of these does, just understand that they take the data coming in from the Web server and put it into a format that is easy for FileMaker to understand.

Part of the ROFM package is a tutorial, including a sample database (all included on this book's CD-ROM). The Scripting Additions also are located in the FileMaker CGI folder. You need to run this tutorial on the Macintosh that you are using as a Web server. To install these, go to the Extensions folder in your System folder. Go to the Scripting Additions folder, drag-and-drop all four Scripting Additions from the CD into that folder, and restart your Macintosh. To use the tutorial, you'll also need the following pieces installed on this Macintosh:

- WebSTAR (the server software from StarNine Technologies)

- FileMaker Pro

- Eudora (the email package from Qualcomm, available from most Macintosh archives)

You can install FileMaker and Eudora on another machine on your local network. This is done frequently to allow the Web server to increase the processing power of one Macintosh and not have to share it with any other applications. Refer to the documents that come with the CGI for more information.

Note

With ROFM, the CGI is free, but the Scripting Additions are not. All four Scripting Additions come from ACME, and if you continue to use ROFM CGI, you'll need to pay for the Scripting Additions.

NetForms

Tab-delimited files separate each piece of information with a tab character. Most databases are able to import tab delimited files and place each piece of information in a different field.

If you are looking for plug-and-play, you can't beat NetForms. NetForms guarantees no programming is required.

NetForms runs native on Power Macs. In addition to taking the data from a form and dumping it into a text file (the text is tab delimited, so you can easily import it into a database), you also can have it formatted as HTML. This way, you can have user-input information posted back up to your Web site and create bulletin-board style discussion areas on your Web site.

A benefit of NetForms is that a company stands behind it. Freeware is great, but it can be a headache trying to get support. You can rely on Maxum to help troubleshoot. You can check out the Maxum Web site at `http://www.maxum.com`.

 Note

NetForms is from Maxum Development. Maxum was the first com-mercial manufacturer of CGIs for the Macintosh, back when WebSTAR was still a shareware product called MacHTTP. NetForms is one of the flagship products.

WebFM

WebFM is another CGI used to interface your Web site with FileMaker Pro. Like ROFM CGI, it is written in AppleScript. WebFM can jump some of the speed hurdles that AppleScript can jump.

Tango

Tango is data capture taken to the next level. It is a complete CGI that enables you to tie Butler—currently the only Standard Query Language (SQL) database for Macintosh—to your Web site. Butler has major potential for handling data and having that power tied to your Web site opens a number of possibilities. In addition to capturing client information, you can publish an entire site from within the database.

Just like the FileMaker CGI, you need to have a Butler database before you can use Tango.

 Note

Everyware Development, the makers of Tango and Butler, have several examples of what can be done with the tools up on their Web site (`http://www.everyware.com`). One example includes a slick online store using a shopping cart metaphor that allows users to click through several pages and pick up products as they go.

NetLink 4D

ACI US manufactures one of the major relational database environments for Macintosh: Fourth Dimension (aka 4D). The 4D environment is a complete programming language, and a number of programmers use it to develop applications.

Some developers, however, have created externals for 4D. These externals are little pieces of software that enable 4D programmers to create complex applications without having to re-write code.

 Note

Externals are similar to the AppleScript Scripting Additions discussed earlier.

ForeSight Technologies has created a 4D external that enables a 4D database to interact with a Macintosh Web server. The software, called NetLink 4D, gives you all the capabilities of having a database integrated into your Web site (allowing users to input data, do finds, and assemble dynamic pages to be published on your site), plus the serious data crunching power of a 4D database.

Imagemap CGIs

It is easy to create imagemaps using PageMill's Image Editor. For those imagemaps to work, however, you need to have a CGI on the server that can process the information that comes in when the mouse is clicked. Currently, two CGIs are on the Internet that will do this processing for you. In addition, Delphic Software's NetAlly Server plans to support imagemaps.

If you have created an imagemap, talk to the Webmaster so that he knows that he'll need to either have a CGI installed that can interpret the map file output by PageMill, or set up his server software to handle image maps.

ImageMap.acgi

ImageMap.acgi comes from Lutz Wiemann. Lutz's CGI is fast, somewhat easy to use, and free. You can download ImageMap at `http://weyl.zib-berlin.de/imagemap/Mac-ImageMap.html`.

You've already seen how to use PageMill to create the map file that contains the coordinates for the imagemap. What ImageMap.acgi does is provide the server with the intelligence to read that map file and tell the server what URLs to serve when a particular coordinate is clicked. This is a prime example of CGIs extending the functionality of the Web server. The server only wants to serve files, not figure out what a set of coordinates means, so it passes that information to the CGI and lets the CGI figure out what it means.

The only difficult part of using ImageMap.acgi is the config file. ImageMap.acgi can handle several different imagemaps provided it knows which map file to use for each one. This is handled is by assigning keywords to each map that match keywords for each map file. You saw how this worked in Chapter 4, "Imagemaps and the Image View," where you included a keyword as a part of the URL when you specified the image as a map.

MapServe

MapServe is another CGI that works similarly to ImageMap.acgi. The basic concept is the same. The Web server software hands off the coordinates returned when a viewer clicks a hot spot on a map to the CGI, the CGI converts that to a URL based on information it has read from a map file, which then hands it back to the Server. MapServe can be downloaded from `http://www.spub.ksu.edu/other/machttp_tools/mapserve`.

The main difference between MapServe, which comes from Kelly Campbell at the University of Kansas, and ImageMap.acgi is that MapServe doesn't use the keyword scheme to locate the map file. Instead, the map file is part of the URL. There really isn't one scheme that is better than another. You decide which one you prefer.

 Note

MapServe has the same great attributes of ImageMap: it's fast, free, and easy to use.

NetAlly

NetAlly is the server software from Delphic Software. Delphic has a vision of a single software package that can handle just about any Internet server requirement that you need. Part of this is built-in support for imagemaps.

If you are using NetAlly you won't need another application to turn the coordinates into a URL; the server will have built-in capability. You still will need to produce the map file, and create a link to it inside the Location box in the Attributes Inspector, but you won't need to install another application.

Email CGIs

The mailto HTML command can be used to create a link to a person's email address (as in `mailto:gary@mactivity.com`). In browsers that have a built-in email client (as Netscape does), this opens a mail message with the person's email address already in the To: field. Unfortunately, not every Web browser has a built-in email client, and therefore does not support the mailto tag. So, if you want to provide the capability to send an email to everyone visiting your site, regardless of whether his or her browser software supports it, you'll need a CGI.

A few email CGIs are available now for Macintosh, some written in AppleScript and some in C. In addition to a Web server, you also need to be running a Simple Mail Transfer Protocol (SMTP) server to use these CGIs. This is because the CGI will create a mail message and send it through your Internet email server. Again, if you are running Delphic's NetAlly, you probably won't need another application because SMTP is part of the package. If you are running any other server, check out the Apple Internet Mail Server(AIMS), which is available from Apple's Web site at `http://www.apple.com`.

SMTP Servers

The application that you use on your desktop machine to send email is a *client*. For the email you write to make its way to another client machine (of the person to whom you sent the email), it needs to first pass through a server. Email servers use one of several different protocols, and one of the more common is SMTP.

Forms.acgi

Forms.acgi is a free CGI (available from `http://www.maxum.com`) that takes the data input from a form (like the ones we created in PageMill), puts it into an email message, and sends it to someone. Most of the configuration for Forms.acgi is done with hidden fields in your form, including names and addresses for both the sender and the receiver, and the subject line. This means that if you want a message to go to different people, you need to create separate fill-in forms for each.

You can further customize with Forms.acgi, but it's a little tricky. Most of the information that is sent with email is stored in the application's resources. The only way to change that information is to use an application called ResEdit.

ResEdit is not for the meek. ResEdit lets you peer deep into the guts of an application and make changes in some of the fundamental ways that the application handles data. Accidentally change a "1" to a "0" and you could destroy your application. Before using ResEdit, read a book on using it (*Zen and the Art of ResEdit* from BMUG is a good one) and make a backup of the application you're about to toy with.

But, you don't need to customize Forms.acgi with ResEdit for it to work. If you like the look of the interface, you're all set!

Email.acgi

Email.acgi is an AppleScript that does the same thing as Forms.acgi. It takes the information from a form and drops it into an email. Email.acgi, like ROFM.cgi, needs a few Scripting Additions (Parse CGI and TCP Scripting Additions, all included on the CD-ROM) to work. Email.acgi can be downloaded from `http://www.lib.ncsa.edu/staff/morgan/e-mail-cgi.html`.

Email.acgi also is totally configured by the form that you create in PageMill. Using hidden fields, you can control who the message is sent to and from, as well as the SMTP server that the message should go to (yes, you do need access to an SMTP server to use this CGI).

Again, your preference will determine whether to use Email.acgi or forms.acgi on your Web site. Email.acgi is written in AppleScript, so it may be a little slower. But, it is easier to customize AppleScripts than to use ResEdit.

Counter CGIs

Counter CGIs simply keep track of how many people have visited a particular site, and shows the reader that number.

Not long ago, it became incredibly popular to have a counter on your Web site's home page. There's no point to this other than to let people know how popular your site is, or to show off your Web know-how (counters require CGIs). If you want to track the number of visitors to your site for marketing or advertising purposes, you should use an application that processes the log file that your Web server produces like ServerStat.

But counters are cool, and fun. The following CGIs for Macintosh are available that enable you to put a counter on your page quickly and easily:

- Count WWWebula

- NetCloak

 Note

ServerStat is an application that will process your log and create an HTML page giving you the vital statistics of your Web site, charting connections by the day and hour, plus telling you how many connections were made from various domains (such as education, commercial, or government). Download ServerStat from http://165.247.199.177/ss.html.

Count WWWebula

Count WWWebula is a shareware package from Kagi Software. Kagi Software is available at http://198.207.242.3/. The counter displayed on your Web page is a GIF image when you are using a

CGI, rather than just a number. A few GIFs come with the package, plus there is a way to have your own GIFs displayed as the numbers. The coolest is an odometer graphic.

Count WWWebula is a C application, and it runs native on PowerMacs. It actually puts up the GIF quickly. Count WWWebula also has a way to disable the counter when your Web site is accessed by certain machines. This is so that your hits to your own Web site don't get counted, only those hits made by others.

NetCloak

NetCloak, from Maxum Development is listed here as a counter CGI, but that really doesn't do it justice. Providing a quick way to display a counter is only a small part of what NetCloak can do. In reality, NetCloak provides about 30 new HTML commands that give you control over what information is displayed on your Web site.

You might be saying, "HTML? I thought the whole point was that I didn't have to write HTML?" This is true, but remember that PageMill does allow you to put HTML commands into your document by assigning text the Raw HTML attribute. If you plan to use NetCloak, you need to format the commands as raw HTML. That is, until Adobe devises a way to integrate NetCloak's tags into the point-and-click PageMill environment.

So, what can NetCloak do besides display a counter? It can have items randomly displayed. It can change the look of your page depending on any number of qualities of the browser software (for example, you can display information to clients viewing from educational sites differently from those viewing from commercial sites). It can even change the information on your page depending on the date or time of day.

NetCloak is made by the same people who make NetForms: Maxum Development. You can download a sample copy of NetCloak from `http://www.maxum.com`.

Searching CGIs

Searchability is a great thing to provide on your site. Whenever you begin gathering large amounts of information, users are going to be frustrated when they can't find exactly what they want quickly. Two CGIs are available for Macintosh Webmasters to enable browsers to search through documents on your site, and both are almost completely plug-and-play.

AppleSearch.acgi

Plug-and-play means that, regardless of what you have installed, you can install the software or plug the device in and use it.

Apple has a powerful document search engine that works over local networks called AppleSearch. Robin Martheus, a programmer at Apple, has released a CGI that enables you to search through AppleSearch archives over the Web.

Using the CGI requires that you have the AppleSearch application either on the same Macintosh as the Web server, or on a Macintosh that is accessible over your network. AppleSearch.acgi has the same problem with custom configuration that Forms.acgi has: you have to poke around in the resource with ResEdit.

 Note

The CGI is free, but AppleSearch is not. AppleSearch does come bundled with the Apple Internet Server Solution. Download the latest version of AppleSearch.acgi from `http://kamaaina.apple.com`.

TR-WWW

TR-WWW (found at `http://www.monash.edu.au/informatics/tr-www.html`) is another solution for providing searching capabilities on your Web site. TR-WWW is a stand-alone application. It searches all documents that you have placed in a particular folder. The advantages of TR-WWW over AppleSearch.acgi are that you don't need another application running in addition to the CGI, and you don't need to prepare the documents to be searched the way that you do with AppleSearch.

The downside is that TR-WWW needs some configuration that is not very intuitive. It has a dreaded config file—a long text file with strange codes that tell TR-WWW how to behave. You also need to create your own form (not so with AppleSearch), but that's easy to do with PageMill.

CGIs for Other Platforms

Of course, CGIs exist for all Web server platforms. If you are in an environment where you are authoring with PageMill on your Macintosh, but have to eventually publish your pages on UNIX or windows machine, you'll not be able to run the CGIs mentioned here.

If you want to use CGIs on your site, the first step is to find out more about the server where your page is eventually going to reside (of course, if you are the Webmaster, this should an easy step). You can start by asking the following two questions.

The first question you should ask is what type of computer the server is running on, and which server software the administer uses. This is important because you need to know what platform the CGI will eventually run on (you can't necessarily run a Windows CGI on a UNIX machine).

The second question to ask is whether you can have CGIs running on the server. Many Web site administrators are wary of allowing users to put CGIs on the server because of the potential for a security breach.

Once you find out what type of machine the CGI will run on, and get permission to actually place a CGI on that machine, there are a couple of Web sites that will help you. Just as we mentioned above, there are several pre-built CGIs that are available for other platforms if you are looking for plug-and-play, and a few tutorials if you are one of the bold pioneers looking to write your own CGIs.

Either way, the best place to start is at Yahoo, the index of Internet sites. Yahoo is arranged by topic, and there is a large list of links to sites with CGI information at:

`http://www.yahoo.com/Computers_and_Internet/Internet/`
`World_Wide_Web/CGI_Common_Gateway_Interface/`

Here is some information for two of the main server platforms, UNIX and Windows.

CGIs for UNIX

There several CGIs available for UNIX servers. You can find a list of some of them at `http://128.172.69.106:8000/cgi-bin/cgis.html`.

At this Web site, you can find a guestbook CGI. Guestbooks are incredibly popular ideas for Web sites. Guestbooks take the information input into a form and captures it to either a text file or a database. The idea is that people can take a minute, fill out a form with their name or email address and some comments about your site.

At this site, you'll also find a CGI that will allow users to add some information to your Web site. This takes the idea of a guestbook to another level: allowing users to enter some information, and have that information posted back up to your Web site. This CGI will enable you to do that on your UNIX Web site.

If you are interested in writing your own UNIX CGIs, there is a tutorial at `http://www.catt.ncsu.edu/~bex/tutor/cgi-bin.html`. This site is specifically advertised as being the place to come if you are a non-programmer, and takes you through the details of CGIs from the very basics, up through writing a simple script.

CGIs for Windows NT Servers

If your Web server runs under Windows NT, and you're looking for a source for CGIs, check `http://rick.wzl.rwth-aachen.de/` `rick/ntweb/index.html`. This is an incredible site, filled with links to both pre-built CGIs, as well as tools that will help you develop your own CGIs.

At this site, you'll find information on Windows NT CGIs that enable you to put counters on your page (with CGI Scripts from Ryan Terry Sammartino or Behold! Software), create forms-based email (with WWWMail from Anthony Moillic or PolyForm from Will Glen Graphics), enable search capabilities (with Web Server Search from Willow Glen Graphics), and create animations (with CycleC32 from Thies Schrader). This site will provide you with jumping off points for these CGIs and more, all running under Windows NT.

If you are interested in writing your own Windows CGIs, you will probably start with a language called Visual Basic. WebLink for Visual Basic is a package which will make this process much easier, especially for novices. Browse `http://ciint1.ciinc.com/vbdemo.htm`.

Summary

CGIs take your Web site to the next level. For a long time, implementing CGIs on your Web site meant that you needed to be a programmer and code them yourself. Today, there are CGIs available that allow you to create imagemaps, interface with databases, and enable readers to search through archives of information; you don't have to program a single line of code. If you want to create your own CGIs, though, there are a number of tutorials which will help you get started.

In the next chapter, you'll learn more about how to add to your Web site. You'll see how to structure your information and make sure that your Web site is easy-to-use, exciting, and fun.

Chapter 6

Web Page Information Architecture Design

By now, you should feel pretty comfortable using PageMill to design and create Web pages that have stylized text, fill-in forms, images, and hypertext links. But remember, thousands of Web pages look terrible because the author understood only the technical details. The Web author needs to know the technical details of presenting a Web page and he needs to think about how viewers will use it. Many of these pages might have great information, but if they are unusable, the information might as well not be presented.

This chapter provides useful information to avoid some of the pitfalls that many first-time Web designers encounter. It also discusses how you can use PageMill's features to help you design powerful, well-designed pages.

Interface Design

Apple Computer, Inc. has an entire department devoted to developing guidelines for building human interfaces. You can peruse their work in *Inside Macintosh: Guide to Human Interface.* When publishing on the Web, you are responsible for creating a human interface, and that is not an easy job. Human interface design is a complex process that includes not only design and layout, but also the way that people interact with information and how they learn.

Interface is a crucial element to every electronic item. An example of bad human interface would be my clock radio. I went from a simple clock with two knobs in the back and a couple of bells to this current clock. It has 15 buttons, 6 of which can change function. I'm expected to understand intuitively the difference between a Sleep button and a Snooze button (I think I snooze on weekends and sleep on weekdays). The manual, which is the size of a small novel, is confusing. I need to use my clock radio, and there aren't any other clock radios immediately available to me, so I have to figure it out.

This is not the case with Web pages. While some might contain crucial information, the bulk of Web pages are just stops along a journey. If you present the viewer with a confusing interface, like my clock radio, it is very likely that they are going to mouse click right past your page.

Good user interfaces provide a friendly, well-thought-out, and easy-to-use way of navigating through information. The Macintosh Finder is an example of good user interface. New users can sit down at a Macintosh and start creating folders, opening files, and using applications in a matter of minutes.

This is what you should strive for with your Web page. You want every new user to navigate through the information on your page, find what he or she wants, and have an enjoyable experience.

Evaluating Web Sites

Start by looking at the first page of your Web site: the home page. This is the entrance to your site—the first text and images that viewers will see when they hit your URL. The best way to think about the design of your site is to consider the purpose of each page. You want to accomplish the following with your home page:

■ Let people know where they are

■ Let people know what type of information they will find

■ Provide links to the rest of your site.

There are, however, at least two other considerations: getting attention and establishing your Web site style. These are a little more difficult to accomplish than the basic goals mentioned here. Look at how a home page can be created when you start with these goals in mind. Take a look at the home page shown in Figure 6.1.

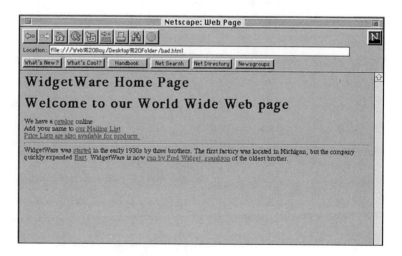

Figure 6.1
Example of a
poorly executed
home page.

Pretty bad, huh? What make this site unusable? The site does let people know where they are: The WidgetWare Home Page. The designer accomplished the first goal.

Unfortunately, he didn't do as well with the second goal; that is, let people know what type of information they can find. There are some links to some other parts of the site, but why would you want to browse a catalog if you had no idea what type of products you were browsing? Occasionally, you can rely on the company name to let people know the type of information they will find on your site, but if you had never heard of StarNine before, would you intuitively know what products they sell?

The designer did score well on the third goal, however. Assuming there are no pages other than the Catalog, Price List, and Mailing List, this page is a good jump point for the rest of the site.

A few of the basic considerations, however, are wrong here. The first cardinal rule of Web site design is: Format your links in a consistent way (see Figure 6.2).

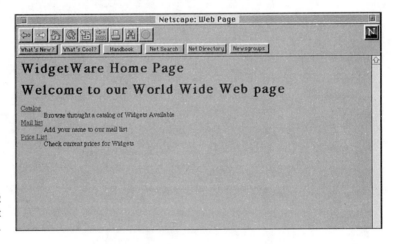

Figure 6.2
Consistently format links.

This page has three links, each formatted a different way. The best way to organize a list of links is to use a list. Start by phrasing each one of your links similarly and remove any "click here" phrases. Your hypertext links should be fully integrated into your Web site. If, for example, you are creating a link to the Apple Web site, make the words "Apple Web site" the link, like this:

```
You can get great Macintosh information from the Apple
Web site.
```

The preceding statement flows better than:

```
You can get great Macintosh information from the Apple
Web site, which you can get to by clicking here.
```

Other than making the text on your site easier to read (by making the sentences much shorter and more concise), phrasing your links in this manner enables people to scan your site quickly to see what links are available.

The type of list that you should use depends on the type of information you are incorporating with your links. For example, if you are just giving pointers with pages that have self-explanatory names, you can use a bulleted list:

- Add your name to our *mailing list*
- Browse our *catalog*
- Check out our *price list*

If you have a description that accompanies the pointers to each page, you can use a definition list, such as this:

■ Mailing List

You can add your name to our mailing list and receive regular updates on our current products, plus news about new product releases.

■ Catalog

You can browse through an online catalog of products, including information on ordering. The catalog also can help you determine if a part is in stock or needs to be ordered.

■ Price List

The online price list reflects the current price of all items, including sales tax for customers within the State of California.

Using Imagemaps

Another technique to use when creating an interface is the imagemap (see Figure 6.3). Using an imagemap enables the viewer—when he or she first connects to your site—to learn immediately what information is available on your site. This has the added benefit of giving you the ability to incorporate your corporation or organization's logo onto the site.

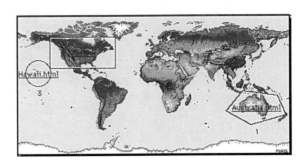

Figure 6.3
An imagemap showing high-lighted areas.

An imagemap is an excellent addition to a home page. If you have a sufficiently exciting image, it also can work to capture the attention of the average mouse potato as he clicks past your site. Imagemaps have the potential to accomplish both of the higher-level goals for a home page: getting attention and establishing a style. PageMill has several tools that help you work with imagemaps. See Chapter 4 for details on how to create imagemaps, and Chapter 5 for details on how to use a CGI to serve imagemaps.

 Note

Many people browse the Web with Images Off to save download time. Therefore, if you create an imagemap you should provide some text links as well so that users will be able to move around your site.

Using Links

Too many fonts is to desktop publishing, what too many links is to Web publishing. Fonts on the Web are controlled almost entirely by the browser—so you can't screw things up that way. In Web publishing, the corollary to too many fonts on a page is too many links. Hypertext is the real power of Web publishing.

 Note

The ability to link documents together was one of the main goals of the development team who created the HyperText Markup Language. The CERN scientists who developed HTML wanted the technology to have the capability to reference one paper to another and a link that would take the reader to that paper.

From the original concept of linking one page to another, you now find paragraphs filled with links that take you to all sorts of pages, sites, and resources. Some of the links might be to pages that are part of the same site; some are to entirely separate sites. Remember that you want your viewers to read and absorb the information on your site. In some instances, several links are appropriate (like a list of someone's favorite sites on her personal page). But for the most part, you should not consider your site as a jump point for the rest of the Web.

When you do want to incorporate links into the body of a paragraph, make sure that the links are meaningful. In WidgetWare, one of the hypertext links is **started**. At first glance, the viewer has no idea what **started** links to. Is it a detailed story about the genesis of the company? Is it a definition of the word started? Who knows? The point of a link is to provide an entry to more information on a particular topic. Make it clear what viewers will find when they follow a particular link; otherwise, there is no compelling reason for them to follow it.

Grouping Links

All hypertext links on your Web site connect to URLs. URLs can point to anything on the Internet, such as other Web pages, gopher sites, ftp sites, or email addresses. There is a tendency when you build links to group items according to the resources from which they originated. An example is grouping all files available via ftp together. This creates a problem for the viewer because it is opposite of how he or she wants to use the site. People get on the Internet to get information, not to use ftp. Therefore, you should group information by topic, not by resource.

Create an Identity

When you enter a store, it's helpful to know where to go to ask questions, or who to talk to when there is a problem. The same thing goes for Web sites—especially commercial Web sites.

Understanding this concept, the creators of HTML have utilized a convenient way for you to accomplish this and it is a feature found in PageMill: the Address attribute. Typically, text at the bottom of a page (usually found below a horizontal rule) includes some information about the person or organization responsible for that page (see Figure 6.4). Enter information you want people to have about your company or yourself (names, phone numbers, mailing or email addresses, fax numbers, and so on) at the bottom of the page and define the text's attribute as Address by selecting Address from the format popup in the Attributes Inspector as (see Figure 6.5).

Figure 6.4
Example of Web-page company information.

Questions? Comments? Contact Mactivity by email at _info@mactivity.com,_ or by phone at 408.354.2500 or 800.798.2928.

Figure 6.5
Address format in the Attributes Inspector.

The text now is italic, raising the question: What's the difference between the Address attribute and the Italics attribute? The answer is somewhat cryptic, but it has to do with what are called *logical* and *physical* tags in HTML. An example of a physical tag is one that makes text bold or italic. It affects the physical look of words. A logical tag is a little different. It is used when you want to classify text as having a specific purpose, such as an address or as a citation from another work. Using Netscape, the Address attribute and the Italics attribute will look the same on-screen. However, that is not true of all browsers. The reason to use logical attributes for an item such as an address is to create consistency from page to page.

You also should make your email address a hypertext link to your email. This is easy to do. Simply highlight the text of your email address and, either at the bottom of the page in the link area or in the Attributes Inspector, attach the URL `mailto:your.email.address`. Now, a viewer can click the email address and, if his browser has a built-in email client, he can send you an email directly.

Creating a Clean, Concise, and Consistent Design

You should present a unified look to your Web site. To create a site that looks like more than just text on a page, you need to establish and follow a plan.

Multimedia designers look at projects as a long process. The first step is to evaluate the purpose of the project. Will it educate, entertain, or distract? The next step is to decide the style of the project. Will it be new wave, traditional, or retro? The next step involves evaluating what resources are available to you such as images, movies, and content. The intended audience also will help determine many of these factors. The multimedia team moves forward only after a concrete plan and a commitment to a defined purpose and style. You need to follow a similar process with your Web site to ensure that it is successful and usable.

The most important thing is to spend time away from the computer before you begin. Do some research and determine who your audience is and what they want. This could be as simple as determining that your audience is your customers and what they want is more information on your product. Or, it could be more complex. For example, your audience might be 8th-grade boys and what they want is to be entertained. Either way, you need to determine what your audience is looking at and whether they are reacting positively or negatively.

The ideal situation is to be able to do a six-month research project with random groups of people in your demographic target audience. That probably won't happen, but you can simply talk to some people who are in your target audience and find out how they feel about the information that is available to them.

Another option is to begin building your site using your best ideas. Find a discussion group on the Internet or online service that deals with your topic, announce your new Web site, and invite people to check it out and provide feedback. You will be amazed at the response you receive. Finally, based on the feedback that you receive, you can begin creating your site and growing it into a full-fledged Web site that functions exactly as you envisioned it.

Web Site Interaction

Web sites are interactive media. The process of following hypertext links is an interactive process. Filling forms is especially interactive. And, just like interaction with people, most viewers become frustrated if your Web site is not responsive to their requests and actions.

Of course, a number of factors, over which you have no control, go into the responsiveness of your Web site. You can't mandate that people use a fast modem, nor can you quit other applications that might be running at the same time as their browser. And you definitely can't make them upgrade to a faster computer.

But you can do a few things to improve your Web site's responsiveness. The first is to ensure that it is continually running. Although most Web server software is extremely reliable, you need to check it occasionally to ensure that the machine has not locked up.

You also can make sure that all your links are good. Nothing is more frustrating for a viewer than clicking on a link and receiving an error message stating that the server could not find a file. Servers are extremely picky when it comes to filenames. One typo in the URL, and your file will never be found. Make sure you test all your links.

You also can play with the settings and preferences on your server software. WebSTAR, for example, enables you to control several aspects of its performance with the WebSTAR administration application. It can optimize performance by determining the number of connections that WebSTAR can handle simultaneously. Adjusting these settings involves some trial and error, but you can experiment to see where you can adjust the settings to get the maximum amount of performance.

Creating Cool Web Sites

The Web is an incredibly exciting technology, and Web sites need to be cool. Creating a site that is clean, neat, and communicates clearly is your primary goal, but interjecting some excitement and jazz also should be a primary consideration to set your site apart from the masses.

Adding Multimedia

The Web is a multimedia environment. You have the capability to incorporate sound, video, and animation into your Web site. Unfortunately, we aren't quite to the point where multimedia can be played as an integrated part of your Web document. For now, you can add hypertext links to movies that can be downloaded to a local hard drive and then played by an external application.

You can serve any QuickTime movie over the Internet. But, you need to flatten it first. (You need to compress the image so that it can be transferred and read by the user. Actually, what it means is that you need to take the two pieces of the file—the resource part and the data part—and put them into the same piece. In official Macintosh terminology, these parts are called *forks*). This is done with a utility called "flattenMooV." It is available in a number of places, but you can find it at http://www.biap.com. To use flattenMooV, double-click to get the standard Macintosh Open file dialog box.

The movie that you are going to flatten must already exist. flattenMooV is not a QuickTime movie creator or editor. It only flattens.

Choose the movie that you want to work with by double-clicking it in the dialog box. The movie will open (see Figure 6.6), and you can preview it by clicking the Play button (the one with the forward arrow on it).

Figure 6.6
Opening a movie.

Close the movie by either clicking the Close box in the upper-left hand corner of the window. flattenMooV is somewhat non-standard in that it has no pull-down menus. When you close the window, you get a dialog box that saves the movie. You'll see in the filename box that the extension .flat has been added to the filename. This does not work well for our purposes in that movies that are transferred over the Internet need an extension that the browser software can recognize. There are a few of these. The extensions for QuickTime movies are .qt or .mov. If you are working with a movie in the MPEG format, you should use .mpeg, mpg, or mpe. Save the new, flat movie with one of these extensions and a filename (remember, it can't have spaces).

Now, back in PageMill, create a link to your movie by choosing an element to be the hypertext link (a word, image, or a region of an imagemap). The URL you should use is `my_movie.mov`. Unfortunately, there's no way to test this in PageMill because PageMill is not aware of helper applications. So, save this file as `movie_test.html` and open it within your browser. When you activate this hypertext link, your helper application in charge of playing movies will open, and the movie will be played. When the viewer activates the link, the movie will be transferred to his or her computer, then played by whatever helper application he or she uses to view movies.

Adding Sounds

Adding sound files to your Web site is easier than adding movies. The process is the same; however, you must create a link to the file and when it is activated, the sound file is transferred to the user's machine and played by a helper application.

Audio files can be created a number of ways, and by using a number of applications. After your file has been created, add an extension that the browser software can recognize. There also are a number of these. Macintosh audio formats use .aif and aifc.

Open PageMill, type the words **Here's a sound!**, and highlight the text. Now create a link to the sound file that you just created (see Figure 6.7) by typing **sound.aif** at the bottom of the page. Now press Return. (You'll need to leave PageMill and go to your browser to test this link.)

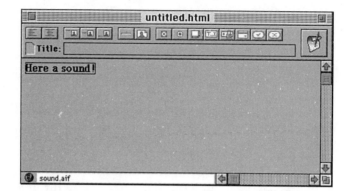

Figure 6.7
Hyperlinking to
a sound file.

Adding Animations

Animations can grant your Web site instant coolness. However,
they are reasonably difficult to finesse. There is very easy way to
post animations, but you need to serve these animations from the
WebSTAR server and view them with the Netscape browser. The
Netscape part is not a big deal because the vast majority of people
use it. But, if you are serving from a platform other than
Macintosh, or are using a server other than WebSTAR, this won't
work.

WebSTAR has the ability to serve a certain type of file called RAW!
files. RAW! files can be used to create simple animations of just a
few frames by encoding all the data for each frame into a part of
the file. When this file is viewed by Netscape, the frames are
shown in order, and you can create simple animations.

The way to create these files is to use an application called
Animaker (written by WebSTAR author Chuck Shotton and
available on StarNine's Web site: http://www.starnine.com).
Animaker enables you to choose several GIF images and output
them as a single RAW! file.

Currently, the only other way to create animations on your Web page is to use a technology called server-push. A typical Web server/client transaction is on in which the client requests the file, the server sends it, and the connection is broken. With server-push transactions, the server keeps the connection open and continues sending data. This enables the server to continually send new frames for animations. Server-push, however, requires a CGI. (RAW! files don't.) If you want to find out more about server-push, see the technical documentation about it on Netscape Communications' Web server: `http://www.netscape.com/assist/net_sites/pushpull.html`.

Looking Forward

A number of technologies are beginning to appear for Web-page designers, technologies that will enable you to put new animation and interactivity on your Web site. The three major technologies to watch right now are:

- Java
- VRML
- Shockwave

Note

Applets are small applications which are meant to be run on a client's computer.

Java is a programming language from Sun Microsystems. Similar to C++, Java enables developers to create applets. The applications are inlined into a standard Web page, meaning that an entire application can be running in the middle of a standard Web page. This is used to do things such as run a live stock market ticker across the top of a page, or create small animations that teach people to juggle. Find out more at `http://java.sun.com`.

VRML (Virtual Reality Modeling Language) is similar to HTML in that it uses just a simple text file that is interpreted by the browser. VRML files, though, describe three dimensional, virtual-reality scenes through which users can navigate. VRML authors also can embed hot links within scenes, which work exactly like hot links on a standard Web page. For more information, check out `http://vrml.wired.com/`.

Shockwave is a technology from Macromedia, the company that created Director, the premier multimedia authoring package. Shockwave enables Webmasters to take Director projects and serve them over the Web. This brings an entire new level of interactivity to Web sites. Expect to see real multimedia on the Web with Shockwave technology in the near future. Find out more at `http://www.macromedia.com`.

Other technologies are on their way. Real Audio, the client/server technology from Progressive Networks, enables Web surfers to listen to audio files in real-time (without having to first download the file), and LiveScript, a scripting language, works with the Netscape Navigator to enable some interactivity (sort of a Java lite). For information on Real Audio, check out `http://www.realaudio.com/`. For info on JavaScript, check out `http://home.netscape.com/comprod/products/navigator/version_2.0/script/index.html`.

Summary

A lot goes into making your Web site a usable resource. Most importantly, you must create an interface that viewers will enjoy using, and one that will help them get to the information that they want. When you do that, you can think about adding more media and more cool features.

Chapter 7

Advanced Tips

By now, you should feel pretty comfortable with PageMill and your abilities to use the software to create Web pages. This chapter covers some of the more advanced techniques and some of the secrets of Webpublishers. It also will look at some of the more technical details of serving pages over the World Wide Web.

Server Platforms

The documents that you create with PageMill can be served and viewed by any computer running Web server software. Because PageMill runs on a Macintosh, you can do all your authoring on a Macintosh, but have those documents served to clients from any computer and any operating system. This section discusses your options for the two most popular Web server operating systems:

- UNIX

- Macintosh

UNIX

UNIX is the traditional operating system for Internet applications. There are a few options for running a Web server under UNIX, but the two most common are NetSite from Netscape Communications and NCSA's httpd.

The good news about NCSA's httpd is that it's free. The software was developed at the National Center for Supercomputing Applications (the same place where the original Mosaic software was born) and is available at `ftp://ftp.ncsa.uiuc.edu/Web/httpd/Unix/ncsa_httpd/current`. The bad news is that this is UNIX, and it is about as far from plug-and-play as it gets. If you don't have a serious background in UNIX programming, you might as well forget about setting up and maintaining a UNIX Web server by yourself. While not impossible, it will take a huge amount of your time. Plus, you'll need to spend some time making sure that the security holes that exist in UNIX are plugged, and plugged correctly.

Note

The problems associated with UNIX are the concerns of the person who is running the Web server. If you are only authoring pages, you don't need to worry about the complexity of UNIX.

Macintosh

By now, you've probably realized this book has a Macintosh bias. Because PageMill runs only on Macintosh, chances are pretty good that you are a strong Macintosh user. If you are not already running a Macintosh server, or you are evaluating which platform to choose for your Web server, think Macintosh. Macintosh computers have the horsepower you need to serve even the busiest sites. Macintosh computers also have the capability to use CGIs to communicate easily with other applications on your hard drive, including databases. Currently, the following three companies market on Macintosh Web servers:

- StarNine Technologies
- InterCon Technologies
- Delphic Software

StarNine Technologies

StarNine is at the top of the hill with WebSTAR. WebSTAR began life as a shareware product known as MacHTTP. In early 1995, StarNine acquired MacHTTP as a product and hired its author, Chuck Shotton. Since that time, StarNine has pushed the development of the product, and it currently reigns as the number one Macintosh Web server. And with good reason. In addition to its power, WebSTAR is significantly less expensive than a UNIX Web server. It also gives you the ease-of-use that Macintosh users have come to expect and love. To create a Web server on a Macintosh (assuming you've already set up your Internet connection), install WebSTAR and double-click it. That's it.

Note

You can find more information about StarNine's WebSTAR, and get a hold of a demo version at `http://www.starnine.com`.

InterCon Technologies

InterCon has a reputation for building TCP/IP applications for the Macintosh, and its TCP/Connect II was one of the first commercial Internet navigation software packages available. Its Web server is dubbed InterServer.

Note

Find out more information and download a demo version of the product at InterCon's Web site: `http://www.intercon.com`.

Delphic Software

Delphic Software soon will release NetAlly, a product that makes extensive use of an Apple networking technology called Open Transport. In addition to being a Web server, NetAlly will perform as an email server, a news server (for the discussion groups on the Internet), and perform a slew of other Internet server tasks. NetAlly has the potential to be a strong all-in-one solution.

Note

You can get more information and updates on the release of NetAlly at `http://www.delphic.com`.

Optimizing Graphics

One of the biggest challenges you will face as you author Web documents is using images. The original plan for the Web did not include images, and support for them is not the Web's strongest feature. Strict guidelines are in place for images that you serve over the Web, and you'll need to follow them closely.

Colors

When you bring an image into PageMill, either by dragging and dropping it onto the page or by inserting it through the dialog boxes, it automatically gets converted to GIF (Graphical Interchange Format) format. GIF is an image format understood by all platforms, so it is especially useful for Web authoring.

GIF's cross-platform capability is definitely a strong point, but it is not without compromises. First, GIFs must have a maximum of eight bits of information per pixel, which limits the number of colors you can have in your image to 256. If you have an image that was created with thousands or millions of colors, expect to see its color quality drop significantly when it goes on the Web.

The problem is further compounded because the computer can only decide which 256 colors it is going to use once per screen. If you have two images on the same page that use two different sets of colors (called palettes), expect the second image to look terrible because the 256 colors have already been chosen.

A tool called the DeBabelizer, however, can help you get out of this jam. The DeBabelizer, from Equilibrium Software, helps you choose the best possible combination of 256 colors for your images.

There is, however, another way to do this using either Adobe Photoshop, the premier image editing application for Macintosh, or a shareware image editing application like Graphic Converter. This is best thought of as a *work-around*, which is computer slang for a solution that is arrived at by finding an unexpected or unusual method.

To do what is called the 256-color work-around, open a new document in either Photoshop or Graphic Converter, and set it to display thousands (or millions, if your monitor is capable) of colors. In separate windows, open all the images that you plan to display on a single Web page. Now, cut and paste each one of those images onto the new page that you have created. You now have a single page with all of your graphics on it.

Reduce the number of colors on that page to 256. In Graphic Converter, this is done by choosing 256 Colors (8 bit) from the Color option in the Picture pull-down menu. In Photoshop, this is done by choosing Index Color from the Mode pull-down menu and choosing the 8 bit/pixel radio button.

Both applications will automatically select the optimum 256 colors to display these images. The last step is to cut and paste these images back into their own windows. Create a new window for each, and save each one.

DPI

The images that are part of your Web site are digital in every sense. They are created (or at least edited) on a computer, served by a computer, and viewed by a computer. Unless users want to print the image, the images never go to paper.

This is both good and bad news for you. The good news is that your image resolution doesn't need to be larger than 72 dpi (dots per inch), because that is the resolution of a computer monitor.

You can create your image, save it, and serve it at a higher dpi, but it will always be displayed at 72 dpi. The higher the dpi, the more memory the image file takes, thus the longer it takes to transfer and display the image to the viewer. So, if you have an image that is 144 dpi, it will transfer at 144, but only display at 72. You might as well save it at 72 and speed up your transfer times.

Unfortunately (and you knew this was coming), there is a trade-off. Having 72 dpi means that your resolution is much rougher than it would be at a higher dpi. If your image is physically large (takes up a large chunk of space of the screen), the jagged, blocky lines that a 72 dpi image has will be much more apparent.

Again, there are some work-arounds available. Try not to serve images that require a large amount of fine detail. If you must serve images with a lot of detail, you need to get a strong image editing application (such as Photoshop) and learn to dither.

Dithering is a process that helps to smooth rough edges by blurring the image's lines. By not trying to create an exact curve, for example, a dithered image fades out the line into the background. The overall effect is that lines are much crisper.

Raw HTML

The final output of PageMill is HTML. HTML is the language that is transmitted over the Web and interpreted by Web browsers, such as Netscape and Mosaic. PageMill outputs HTML because it is the only language currently understood by Web browsers.

 Although PageMill does not require that you write HTML, it does exist in PageMill files. If you open any sample files ending with .html in a text editor (SimpleText or TeachText), you can see Raw HTML as shown in Figure 7.1.

```
<HTML>
<HEAD>
    <TITLE>Continents Page</TITLE>
</HEAD>
<BODY BACKGROUND="../EarthAndWareTutorial/images/paper1.gif">
<IMG SRC="../Images/image9.gif" WIDTH="465" HEIGHT="60"
ALIGN=bottom NATURALSIZEFLAG=
"0" BORDER="3">
<H2><CENTER>Welcome to the Continent Explorer Page</CENTER>
</H2>
<BR>
<BR>
The Continents Explorer Page is the resource for finding out
more about the seven continents, as well as the place to
share your experiences travelling around the world.<BR>
<A HREF="map.html"><VAR></VAR></A>
<MENU><A HREF="map.html">Continent Facts</A> <BR>
This page contains a clickable map of the world and
information about the continents <BR>
<A HREF="form.html">Explorer History</A> <BR>
```

Figure 7.1
Example of a Raw
HTML file.

If you look closely, you'll see the text that is displayed on-screen in the Web browser when this page is transmitted over the Web. Codes within angle brackets (< >) surround the text. The codes in those brackets are HTML. In HTML, these codes are called *tags*. These tags turn on and off certain attributes. For example, a few lines from the top of the document, you should see the line:

```
<H1>This is a sample heading</H1>
```

The text This is a sample heading is displayed in the largest heading attribute when viewed by a Web browser. When you view this file with SimpleText, you see instructions to the Web browser on how to display the text. The <H1> tag is a message to the Web browser to begin displaying text as the largest heading. The </H1> tag is a message to stop displaying text as the largest heading.

 Note

> HTML tags usually are typed in capital letters. There is no technical reason for this; the tags work the same regardless of whether they are in upper- or lower-case. This is only done to help HTML authors pick the tags from the text that is to be displayed.

Of course, with PageMill, all you need to do is type **This is a sample heading** in the main window (make sure you are in Edit mode), select the text with the pointer, and choose the Largest Heading attribute (from the Format menu or in the Attributes Inspector). PageMill places the tags for you.

But suppose you want to add some HTML code that you read about in a magazine or learned at a Web building seminar? Maybe some code that is not yet supported by PageMill? Netscape Communications, for example, is constantly expanding the HTML language, adding tags that format text and images in several ways. Although PageMill does enable you to put some of these Netscape-isms into your pages (such as changing the background color of your page), it does not let you use all of them. For example, you cannot use PageMill to create tables. The only way to to use table tags (in this version, that is) is by inputting the HTML onto your page and designating it as Raw HTML.

Create a simple table and designate it as Raw HTML. If you have never written HTML before, much of this will be cryptic. Because you have decided to use PageMill as an authoring tool, you really don't need to know much about HTML. If you want to learn more about Netscape's extensions to HTML, however, check out http:/ /www.netscape.com.

Open a new page in PageMill (⌘-N). (Make sure you are in Edit mode). Now, type the raw HTML; you'll designate it as HTML when you are done. First type the tag for building a table:

```
<TABLE>
```

As in the heading example earlier, you'll need to tell the browser software when you are done building the table. This is done with the `</TABLE>` tag. Go down four lines and enter the `</TABLE>` tag:

```
<TABLE>

</TABLE>
```

When using the `</TABLE>` tag, you also need to specify whether you want to have a border around your table. To include a border, change the tag to `<TABLE BORDER>` (don't change the closing tag). You also can increase the width of the border by specifying how many pixels wide you would like it to be (for example, `<TABLE BORDER=5>` would create a table with a five pixel border).

`<TR>`, which stands for table row, is the tag that starts a new line. The table you're going to create is going to have two rows and three columns. To build the first row, start by first entering the tag for a new table:

```
<TABLE BORDER>
<TR>

</TABLE>
```

You'll also need to close the `<TR>` tag. (Now can you see why no one really enjoys writing HTML?) Give yourself some space for the next step—putting information into the table's cells—and close the `<TR>` with the `</TR>` tag, for example:

```
<TABLE BORDER>
<TR>                          </TR>
</TABLE>
```

Now, add some information to the cells of the table. <TD> is the tag used to designate information that is to be displayed as a cell within a table. Enter the <TD> tag after the <TR> tag, for example:

```
<TABLE BORDER>
<TR><TD>Item #1                </TR>
</TABLE>
```

Just as the <TABLE> and the <TR> tags need to be closed, so does the <TD> tag. Use the </TD> tag to close a cell of a table, for example:

```
<TABLE BORDER>
<TR><TD>Item #1</TD>           </TR>
</TABLE>
```

All of the information within the <TD> and </TD> tags will be displayed as a single cell within your table. You can create as many cells as you want, as long as you put the information between a <TD> and a </TD> tag. For this example do three:

```
<TABLE BORDER>
<TR><TD>Item #1</TD><TD>Item #2</TD><TD>Item #3</TD></TR>
</TABLE>
```

You can create as many rows as you like, as long as you put the information between a <TR> and a </TR> tag. In this example, make two rows:

```
<TABLE BORDER>
<TR><TD>Item #1</TD><TD>Item #2</TD><TD>Item #3</TD></TR>
<TR><TD>Item #4</TD><TD>Item #5</TD><TD>Item#6</TD></TR>
</TABLE>
```

This is a complete table. If you try to save this as it is, PageMill will try to put it into a format it understands. However, you want PageMill to leave it alone, because you know that the browser software will interpret it and display it as a table. So, you want to save it as Raw HTML.

Use your mouse and highlight the text (as in Figure 7.2). Open the Attributes Inspector by either selecting it from the View pull-down menu or by pressing ⌘-;. Select the Raw HTML box in the lower left corner of the Page mode of the Attributes Inspector. The HTML that you typed turns red. Now save this file as tables.html.

You can't test this file in PageMill to see if your HTML worked, because PageMill doesn't understand the tags for building tables. Quit PageMill and open Netscape. You have to view this file in Netscape, because it's the only browser that understands the tags for building tables. Don't worry about putting this file on your Web server to view it, you can use any Web browser to view files locally. In the browser, choose Open File from the File menu. Find tables.html in the dialog box that appears. Double-click to open the file and a table appears (see Figure 7.3).

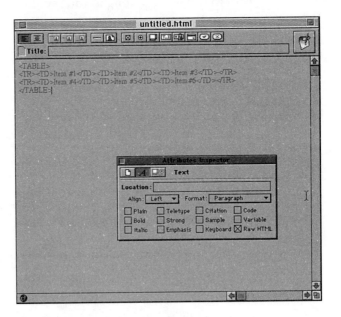

Figure 7.2
Using Raw HTML in PageMill to produce a table.

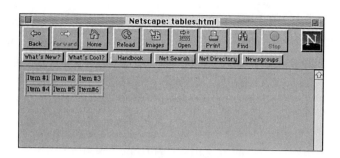

Figure 7.3
Table coding
viewed with
Netscape Navigator.

This is just one example of how you can use the Raw HTML attribute to add formatting elements to your Web page that PageMill doesn't yet support. There are a few others, mostly extensions to HTML from companies like Netscape. Another example is the <FONT SIZE> tag, which enables you to control the size of the characters on your Web page. You can, for example, create a *drop cap effect* (where the first letter of a page is larger than the rest) by typing:

```
<FONT SIZE=6>T</FONT><FONT SIZE=4>his is an example of a drop
cap</FONT>
```

This line, on the Netscape Navigator, will display the first character (the "T") six point sizes larger than the default text size as set by the browser. The rest of the text will be displayed four point sizes larger.

Another effect is displaying text next to an image. To do this, however, you have to forget about the easy, drag-and-drop method of bringing images into your PageMill document. You will have to use the HTML tag used to bring in images.

The HTML tag for bringing in an image is <IMG SRC>. Unlike the table tags and the tag to increase font size, the <IMG SRC> tag does not need to be followed by a closing tag. The name of the image file goes inside this tag, like this:

```
<IMG SRC=boots.gif>
```

With PageMill, you can put one line of text next to an image. It is impossible, however, to have paragraphs of text flow alongside an image. To do this, you must use the Raw HTML command to specify the image's alignment. To align the image along the left margin, you would type:

`<IMG SRC=boots.gif ALIGN=LEFT>`

Now, if you insert some text after this tag, it will flow alongside the image:

`<IMG SRC=boots.gif ALIGN=LEFT>` **This is an image of a pair of boots that was used in our tutorial. The image works well for this example, because it is small and gives us plenty of room to type in some text.**

The tag is the only part that needs to be designated as HTML. When this page is displayed with Netscape, it looks like Figure 7.4.

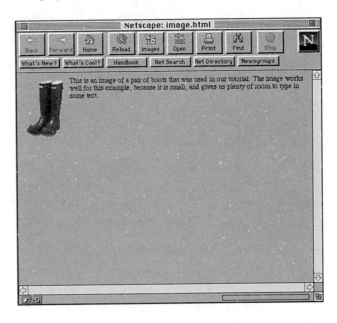

Figure 7.4
Displaying text around an image as viewed in Netscape Navigator.

Summary

Most of what people know about building Web pages comes from experience. The learning curve on the Web is extremely steep. After you have a strong grasp of the basics, you can begin to move rather quickly.

Chapter 8

Looking Forward

"To infinity and beyond."

Buzz Lightyear, *Toy Story*

PageMill has changed the face of Webpublishing. Response to the initial release of the product has been very favorable. But as is the case with most technological innovations, competition is just around the corner. In addition to the standard bug fixes and improvement performances PageMill will inevitably provide, you can look forward to the introduction of a variety of features. Here's a brief discussion on some of the major areas that PageMill will need to address.

HTML Support

It's difficult for a product such as PageMill, which tries to put a graphical interface to text-based HTML, to navigate the evolving environment of HTML standards and extensions introduced by private companies such as Netscape and Microsoft. PageMill probably will evolve to support a *plug-in architecture.* That is, PageMill will ship with a standard functionality and gain additional functionality and support for HTML extensions by adding plug-in software modules. Plug-ins could mimic other browsers' characteristics, support new technologies (such as Sun's Java programming language, the Virtual Reality Modeling Language (VRML) for creating virtual reality-based Web pages, Macromedia's Shockwave, or Apple's QuickTime for adding multimedia capabilities to a Web page), or simply the latest additions to the HTML standard.

Direct Support for Tables

One of the most popular extensions to HTML has been the Netscape extension for tables. Tables provide a simple way to provide rows and columns of text and graphics on a Web page. *The PageMill Handbook* CD-ROM includes a simple utility that you can use with FileMaker and some raw HTML to create tables in PageMill. Many users have requested direct support for tables within the program; it wouldn't surprise us to find this capability available in PageMill's next release.

Enhanced Browser Capability

Look for PageMill's Preview mode to be enhanced in several ways. The browser needs to interpret more HTML extensions and the current HTML standard in a more consistent manner. Some advanced users have taken PageMill to task for the HTML that the program produces. To make the authoring environment more useful, PageMill could provide the capability to see what your page looks like on other browsers. (Remember there are differences in the way different browsers display pages. This could be achieved via a plug-in architecture that would launch other browsers or by mimicking popular browsers in Preview mode.) The Preview mode also could be enhanced to become a fully functioning Internet browser. Wouldn't it be great to surf the Net with your PageMill browser and pick up graphics and hypertext links in cyberspace for use in your Web projects without launching multiple programs? At the very least, PageMill should support browser Helper Applications that can be launched in Preview mode when different file types are called by the Web page. PageMill also should enable you to view your finished Web page and how it will function.

SiteMill

As you quickly will learn, Web projects adhere to the old adage, "Work expands to fit the space you give it."

You'll add additional pages to your Web project on a constant basis. Projects over 50 pages are not uncommon. With the addition of pages and images comes a complexity that becomes difficult to manage. Maintaining hypertext link integrity as you change names or reorganize your Web site can be a challenge for even the most experienced Webpublisher.

In much the same way that PageMill provided a practical interface for creating Web pages, a forthcoming product from Adobe Systems called SiteMill will revolutionize the process for managing

Web sites. SiteMill, due in the first quarter of 1996, will be for users who want to add site management capabilities to their Webpublishers toolbelt. When you paste a link, rename a file, delete a file, or move a file between folders the program automatically updates all links so that they point to the correct location.

SiteMill provides the following capabilities:

- Analyze the integrity of existing Web sites; informs you of any bad links and the ability to resolve them with the click of a button

- Show all resources, page titles, and folders

- Show warnings for unreachable or unused resources

- Automatically fix all links throughout a local site when files or folders are renamed, moved between folders, or deleted

- Enable link creation by simply dropping a resource from the Site view into a page

In addition, the Error view shows all bad links and allows one-step correction. The External References view shows all references to external Web sites and provides for global renaming and updating. The External References view also supports drag-and-drop for easy link creation with other pages.

SiteMill's New Modes

SiteMill combines site management functionality with PageMill's editing environment by adding three new views to PageMill's Edit and Preview modes. These three views are

- Site view

- Error view

- External References view

Site View

Site view (see Figure 8.1) shows you all site resources at a glance: pages, images, directories, scripts, and other files. Pages and images can be opened directly from this view for editing. The visual folder hierarchy enables resources to be named, deleted, and moved between folders. Hypertext links are automatically updated when these actions are taken. Each resource listed includes a popup menu that identifies inbound and outbound links for easy site navigation. Unreachable or unused resources are highlighted in a different color and are easily identifiable. Page and Image icons in the Site view can be dragged onto pages to create hypertext links and insert graphics, respectively.

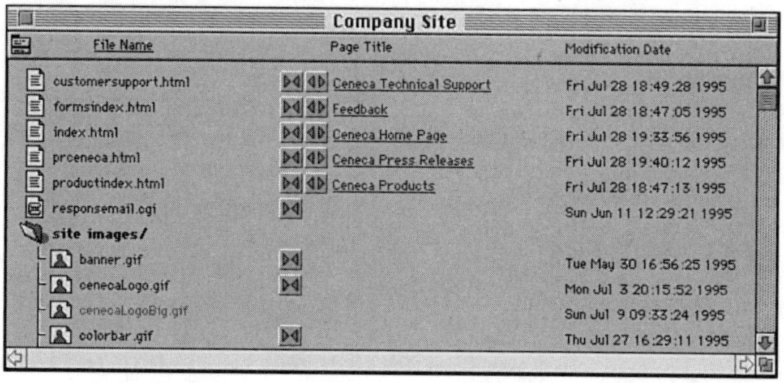

Figure 8.1
SiteMill's Site view.

File Name	Page Title	Modification Date
customersupport.html	Ceneca Technical Support	Fri Jul 28 18:49:28 1995
formsindex.html	Feedback	Fri Jul 28 18:47:05 1995
index.html	Ceneca Home Page	Fri Jul 28 19:33:56 1995
prceneca.html	Ceneca Press Releases	Fri Jul 28 19:40:12 1995
productindex.html	Ceneca Products	Fri Jul 28 18:47:13 1995
responsemail.cgi		Sun Jun 11 12:29:21 1995
site images/		
banner.gif		Tue May 30 16:56:25 1995
cenecaLogo.gif		Mon Jul 3 20:15:52 1995
cenecaLogoBig.gif		Sun Jul 9 09:33:24 1995
colorbar.gif		Thu Jul 27 16:29:11 1995

Company Site

Error View

The Error view, as shown in Figure 8.2, is used for performing repairs on locally maintained, existing sites. This view enables you to identify all link references that are out-of-date and don't resolve correctly. You'll be presented with a list of links that need to be fixed and instructions for correcting them.

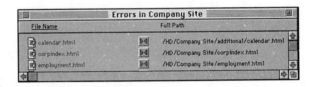

Figure 8.2
SiteMill's Error view.

External References View

The External References view as shown in Figure 8.3 manages your hypertext links to pages on the Internet. In this view, you can ensure that any links you make are accurate and reachable.

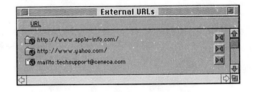

Figure 8.3
SiteMill's External References view.

Summary

Now that you've covered all the program's components and how they work, where do you go from here? Decide if the pages you are creating serve your needs for putting your information on the Web. If you want to continue your education, check out some of the HTML resources recommended in the appendix.

The next frontier for Webpublishers will be the inclusion of new data types such as Java, VRML, and Shockwave into their web pages. You might not create this data yourself, but you'll need to understand what they are and how to use them to build Web pages around them. Another area where Webpublishers can enhance their skills is understanding graphic formats and utilities. Learn everything there is to know about using graphics and you'll be able to design more attractive Web pages.

Appendix A

Command Summary

This appendix provides Macintosh commands for use with PageMill. When available, a command key equivalent is provided next to the command name.

File Menu

Command	Action
New Page (⌘-N)	Starts a new Web page.
Open (⌘-O)	Opens an existing HTML, GIF, or JPEG file.
Close (⌘-W)	Closes the current window.
Save (⌘-S)	Saves the current page or image to disk.
	When saving a Web page, PageMill offers the .HTML file extension.

continues

File Menu Continued

Command	Action
Save As...	Saves a copy of the current Web page or image file under a new name.
Save a Copy As...	Saves a copy of the current page or image file with the file name filename_copy.HTML.
Revert to Saved	Returns to the last saved version of the current page.
Page Setup	Sets printing options.
Print (⌘-P)	Prints the current page.
Quit (⌘-Q)	Exits from PageMill.

Edit Menu

Command	Action
Undo (⌘-Z)	Reverses your last action.
Cut (⌘-X)	Removes selected item from the page and places it on the Clipboard.
Copy (⌘-C)	Places a copy of the selected item on the Clipboard.

Command	Action
Paste (⌘-V)	Inserts the contents of the Clipboard in your document.
Clear	Deletes the selected item.
Select All (⌘-A)	Selects all elements on the current page.
Remove Link (⌘-R)	Removes a URL from selected text or image.
Show/Hide Anchors (⌘-,)	Turns on or off the ability to see anchor markers when editing a page.
Preferences	
General Preferences	Toggles on and off the audibile page flipping sound.
Page Preferences	Selects between Macintosh, UNIX, and DOS line break formats. Selects between .html or .htm for the default file suffix.
Image Preferences	Specifies the default folder to which the images will be saved. Selects whether to use NCSA or CERN imagemap formats. Specifies the root folder for your local editing machine and your remote server, to create proper imagemap files.

Style Menu

Command	Action	HTML Equivalent
Plain (⌘-Shift-P)	Turns text to Plain text (this is the default style).	
Bold (⌘-B)	Turns text to Bold text.	<B></B>
Italic (⌘-I)	Turns text to Italic text.	<I></I>
Teletype (⌘-Shift-T)	Turns text to monospace (typewriter) font.	<TT></TT>
Strong (⌘-Shift-S)	Displays text as bold in PageMill, but could be different on other browsers.	<STRONG></STRONG>
Emphasis (⌘-Shift-E)	Displays text as italic in PageMill, but could be different on other browsers.	<EM></EM>
Citation (⌘-Shift-C)	Displays text as italic in PageMill, but could be different on other browsers.	<CITE></CITE>

Command	Action	HTML Equivalent
Sample (⌘-Shift-A)	Displays text as monospace font in PageMill, but could be different on other browsers.	\<SAMP\>\</SAMP\>
Keyboard (⌘-Shift-K)	Displays text as monospace font in PageMill, but could be different on other browsers.	\<KBD\>\</KBD\>
Code (⌘-Shift-O)	Displays text as monospace font in PageMill, but could be different on other browsers.	\<CODE\> \</CODE\>
Variable (⌘-Shift-V)	Displays text as italic in PageMill, but could be different on other browsers.	\<VAR\>\</VAR\>
Raw HTML (⌘-Shift-H)	Identifies HTML tags that you have entered manually. These tags appear in red. They are not visible in Preview mode.	

Format Menu

Command	Action	HTML Equivalent
Indent Left (⌘-[)	Moves the selected paragraph to the left.	
Indent Right (⌘-])	Moves the selected paragraph to the right.	\<BLOCKQUOTE\>
Paragraph (Cmd-Opt-P)	Removes another format from selected paragraph and returns it to Plain style.	\<BR\>\<BR\>
Heading	Enables you to select a heading size.	
Smallest (⌘-Opt-6)		\<H6\>\</H6\>
Smaller (⌘-Opt-5)		\<H5\>\</H5\>
Small (⌘-Opt-4)		\<H4\>\</H4\>
Large (Cmd-Opt-3)		\<H3\>\</H3\>
Larger (Cmd-Opt-2)		\<H2\>\</H2\>
Largest (Cmd-Opt-1)		\<H1\>\</H1\>
Preformatted (Cmd-Opt-F)	Displays text in a monospace font; keeps text spacing and carriage returns intact.	\<PRE\>\</PRE\>

Command	Action	HTML Equivalent
Address (⌘-Opt-A)	Displays in italic in PageMill.	<ADDRESS> </ADDRESS>
List	Enables you to choose from six list formats.	
Bullet		<UL><LI></UL>
Directory		<DIR><LI></DIR>
Menu		<MENU> </MENU>
Numbered		<OL><LI></OL>
Definition		<DL><DD></DL>
Term		<DT>

Window Menu

Command	Action
Show Pasteboard (⌘-/)	Displays the PageMill pasteboard, a multi-page holding area for text, links, graphics, and form elements.
Show Attributes Inspector (⌘-;)	Displays the Attributes Inspector, a control panel for assigning attributes to various page, text, image, and form elements.
Stack	Used when working with multiple windows simultaneously; displays windows in a cascading style leaving the title bars of each window visible.

continues

Window Menu Continued

Command	Action
Tile	Used when working with mutliple windows; tiles all open windows, sizing them all to fit on the screen.
Close All	Close all open windows.
Open Windows List	Displays a list of open windows. If you have changed a window's content but haven't saved it yet, the window's name appears underlined. Selecting a window from the list makes it the active window.

Miscellaneous Command Keys

Command Key	Action
⌘-Ctrl-spacebar	Toggles the browse button.
⌘-Ctrl-←	Aligns text to the left.
⌘-Ctrl-∏	Aligns text to the right.
⌘-Ctrl-↑	Top aligns images.
⌘-Ctrl-↓	Bottom aligns images.
⌘-Ctrl-1	Activates the Horizontal Rule button.
⌘-Ctrl-2	Activates the Insert Image button.
⌘-Ctrl-3,4,5,6,7,8,9,0	Activates the Insert Element buttons.

Appendix B

Tool Bar Summary

This appendix provides a detailed view of the tool bar available in PageMill. Icons are provided as a visual reference.

Ctrl-Command-C or Ctrl-Command-Enter = Places cursor in the Link Location bar.

Button	Action	HTML Equivalent	PageMill
	Left Align Text	No HTML Equivalent PageMill and HTML default	Ctrl-Command \ Ctrl-Command Left Arrow
	Center Align Text	\<CENTER\>\</CENTER\>	Ctrl-Command] Ctrl-Command Right Arrow
	Top Align Image (text next to image)	ALIGN=top	
	Center Align Image (text next to image)	ALIGN=middle	
	Bottom Align Image (text next to image)	ALIGN=bottom	
	Insert Horizontal Rule	\<HR\>	Ctrl-Command 1
	Insert Image	\<IMG SRC=" path/filename"WIDTH="XX" HEIGHT="XX" NATURALSIZEFLAG="X"ALIGN=bottom\>	Ctrl-Command 2
	Insert Checkbox	\<INPUT TYPE="checkbox" NAME="checkbox" VALUE="checkbox"\>	Ctrl-Command 3

Button	Action	HTML Equivalent	PageMill
	Insert Radio Button	`<INPUT TYPE="radio" VALUE="radio"Button NAME="radio30327" CHECKED="true">`	Ctrl-Command 4
	Insert Text Area	`<TEXTAREA NAME= "name" ROWS="1" COLS="12"></TEXTAREA>`	Ctrl-Command 5
	Insert Text Field	`<INPUT NAME="name" TYPE="text" SIZE="30">`	Ctrl-Command 6
	Insert Password Field	`<INPUT NAME="name" TYPE="password" SIZE="30">`	Ctrl-Command 7
	Insert Popup	`<SELECT> <OPTIONSELECTED> item one <OPTION>item two <OPTION>item three</SELECT>`	Ctrl-Command 8
	Insert Submit Button	`<INPUT NAME="name" TYPE="submit" VALUE= "Submit">`	Ctrl-Command 9
	Insert Reset Button	`<INPUT NAME="name" TYPE="reset" VALUE="Reset">`	Ctrl-Command 0

Action	PageMill
Toggle between Preview/Edit mode	Ctrl-Command Spacebar
Toggle between bottom align and middle align text to image	Ctrl-Command -
Top align text to image (select image first) Note: If text is already top aligned, this command will center align text to image	Ctrl-Command Up Arrow
Bottom align text to image (select image first) Note: If text is already bottom aligned, this command will center align text to image	Ctrl-Command Down Arrow

Glossary

A

Absolute Path Name: A detailed and explicit way of locating a file or device on a network by starting with the name of the computer on which the object or file resides, and then listing any intermediate folders or directories, thus ending with the name of the file or object. For example, `<http://upubs-71.uchicago.edu/wwwbook/appendixes/glossary.html>`.

Acrobat: Portable document software developed by Adobe Systems, Inc. It enables a user to save a file as read-only and enables any number of users to view the file with the free reader utility. Users cannot change text.

Address: The location of a computer, file, or other object on a network (as in FTP address).

America Online: Commercial online service.

Anchor: A hypertext link created in an HTML document. For example, `<A HREF="http://www.mycomputer.com/files/doc.html">Clickable text goes here</A>`.

Anonymous FTP: FTP (File Transfer Protocol) is a common way to connect to a network, access directories, or obtain files. It uses TCP/IP commands, and usually requires a username and a password. Anonymous FTP enables users to log in to remote FTP sites as guests without requiring a password.

AppleScript: 1) An Apple system extension. 2) Apple's scripting language, which creates an interface between Apple Events and scriptable programs. Distributed with System 7.5.

Applet: Program written in the Java programming language that executes within an HTML document displayed by a World Wide Web browser.

Aretha: The current freeware release of the Frontier scripting tool by Dave Winer. Frontier is a scripting environment that enables you to control scriptable Macintosh applications.

ARPAnet: The original name for the Internet, which was developed in 1969 by the Advanced Research Projects Agency of the U.S. Department of Defense (ARPA).

ASCII: American Standard Code for Information Interchange. Pronounced "ask-ee." Computers don't know what letters or numbers are; they recognize only bits of information—zeros and ones. ASCII is binary code that represents characters. It enables computers to display, transmit, and print textual information.

AU: A type of sound file format.

B

Bandwidth: The capacity of a computer channel or data transmission cable, often expressed in bits or bytes per second.

Bin: Abbreviation for binary. Binary means "made up of two parts." All input to a computer is binary, made up of combinations of 0 and 1 data bits. Binary is also a techie term for a computer program. "bin" is often used in "cgi-bin," a commonly used name for a folder/directory where binary files such as CGIs are stored.

Binhex: A method of encoding files from 8-bit to 7-bit format while preserving file attributes.

Bitmap: A binary representation of a graphic object created by translating the object into pixels. Pixels are computerized dots, each of which represents a binary bit of information. In a black-and-white bitmap, for instance, white is on and black is off.

Bookmark: A record of the URL of a Web page you have visited.

Boolean Queries: Feature of a Wide Area Information Server (WAIS) that provides a search for two related keywords joined by the Boolean operators *and, or,* or *not* that appear in a search string.

Browser: A program designed to read HTML files and retrieve and display information on the World Wide Web. Also called a client. *Graphical browsers* have the capacity to display images, colors, and other graphic elements. *Non-graphical browsers* display textual information but not graphics. (See *Netscape Navigator* and *Mosaic.*)

C

Cache: A part of computer memory that can be reserved for storing/processing a specific type of data.

Cell: An alternative term for "frame."

CERN: The European Laboratory for Particle Physics, where the World Wide Web was created.

Certificate: Document issued by a certifying agency that attests that the owner of the key to a Web page has proved authentic identity.

Certificate Information: Information on a Web page that tells you about a page's origin as well as its security status.

CGI: Common Gateway Interface. A standard interface between a Web server and an external (or "gateway") program such as a Web browser. A program that handles a request for information and returns information or performs a search or other routine. Can be written in a number of programs—on the Mac, most CGIs are written in MacPerl or AppleScript.

Character Styles: HTML tags used to add emphasis to specific words, rather than paragraphs, such as <B> </B> for bold, <I> </I> for italic, and so on.

Clickable Imagemap: See *imagemap.*

Client: A synonym for browser. A program that reads and navigates through the Web and retrieves files. (See *browser.*)

Client Pull: One way of creating dynamic documents in which data on a Web server is reloaded after a specified amount of time by "pulling" the data from the server to your browser.

Client-Side Imagemap: An imagemap (see *imagemap)* that processes mouse clicks and accesses URLs on the user's own computer, rather than by doing the processing on the Web server's remote computer, and thus works faster and better than a server-side imagemap.

Cobweb Site: A Web site that has not been updated for a substantial length of time and whose contents are obviously out of date. It is considered bad form to let your site become a "cobweb site."

Common Ground: Portable document software developed by Common Ground Software. It enables a user to save a file as read-only and to enable any number of users to view the file with the free reader utility. Users cannot change text.

Compression: A scheme that makes files smaller, usually by finding a pattern and substituting shorthand for the pattern.

Continuous Document Streaming: Instead of waiting for a document to be assembled *in toto* on your computer before it is displayed, the data is sent to your screen much more quickly and appears in stages.

.CPT: A filename extension that denotes a file created by the shareware program CompactPro.

Cyberspace: A term originally used in the novel *Neuromancer* by William Gibson to describe a computer network of the future that can be connected directly to peoples' minds. Now represents the Internet and/or the Web.

D

Digital Signature: A way for a certifying agency to sign an X.509 or other type of security certificate.

Disk Cache: A part of a computer's disk space set aside for storing/processing information.

Division: A significant section of a long HTML document, such as an appendix or glossary, and designated in HTML 3.0 by the <DIV CLASS=*name*> element.

DNS: Can stand for 1) Domain Name System; 2) Domain Name Service; 3) Domain Name Server. (See *domain name system or service* and *domain name.*)

Document Information: A window that displays general information, such as location and security status, about the Web page onscreen.

Domain Name: A textual alias for an IP address based on the domain name system. Components of a domain name are separated by a period. For example, an IP address for a computer might be 197.99.87.99; it might then have several aliases, one of which is www.mycomputer.com.

Domain Name Server: A computer that keeps track of addresses in a given organization or domain and routes requests to specific addresses.

Domain Name System or Service: A way of distributing information worldwide across the Internet so that no one computer, person, or organization has to keep track of everyone in the world. Instead, computers are assigned standard types of names depending on their domain, and domain name servers share information about their specific area with other computers. Computers in educational institutions are given names ending in the suffix .EDU, governmental offices have the suffix .GOV, commercial ones end in .COM, and so on.

Download: The act of copying a file from the Internet to your computer.

E

Easter Egg: A hidden message, graphic, or other feature built into a program that users discover by typing or choosing undocumented commands.

Encoding: A way of translating Mac files that enables them to be served from a non-Macintosh platform.

EPS: Encapsulated PostScript. (See *PostScript.*)

External Image: An image that is not an inline image and thus part of an HTML document, but that resides in a separate file and is accessed by means of a hypertext link.

F

FAQs: Frequently Asked Questions. FAQs are often seen as sections of Web sites or as updated files posted to newsgroups or servers. They answer the most common questions on a certain topic. It's considered poor form to ask a question that's covered in a FAQ.

Firewall: A security system that restricts traffic between a secure network and the outside world. The secure host machine is the only computer in an organization actually connected to the Internet. Everyone in the organization must go through the host machine to connect to the Internet, and vice versa.

Fixed-Width Fonts: Fonts that have distorted letters so that they are all of the same width.

Flame: A "heated" message from a fellow surfer in regard to a breach of "netiquette" on your part.

Font: A set of characters that, together, make up a typeface such as Times or Helvetica.

Fonts: Netscape Preferences: General dialog box that enables the user to change the font used to display text.

Frame Relay: High-speed packet switching protocol suited for data image transfer. Used with WANs (Wide Area Networks). Not the most efficient way of transmitting real-time voice and video.

Freeware: Software created by independent technoids and available to users free of charge by downloading it from the Internet or from local areas. (See *Shareware.*)

Frontier: A scripting environment for the Macintosh.

FTP: File Transfer Protocol, a method for transferring files to and from remote computers on the Internet. (See *Anonymous FTP.*)

G

GIF: Graphics Interchange Format, a file format commonly used with graphics or photos displayed on Web documents.

Global History File: File that includes a record of all the Web sites you've visited since the last time the Global History File was updated.

Gopher: A text-only, menu-driven Internet information system developed at the University of Minnesota that preceded the Web. It's still very common, and most Web browsers can connect to Gopher servers.

Graphical User Interface: A browser program, such as Netscape, that provides a way for an individual user to graphically view the masses of information on the Internet, with inline or external images, sounds, buttons, icons, and so on.

.GZ: Filename extension for a file compressed with the application Gnu Zip.

H

History: A Netscape command (under the Window menu) that brings up a window containing many (not all) of the Web pages you have visited in the current session.

Hit Counter: A script on a Web server that calculates each "hit" or visit to a Web page every time a connection is made, and displays the current total on the page to the current user.

Home Page: The welcome page of a Web site, the place where visitors are supposed to start when finding out about a particular site.

HotJava: Dynamic Web browser developed by Sun Microsystems, Inc. that uses Sun's Java programming language. HotJava can execute "applets" or programs written in Java that can be included in HTML documents.

HREF Link: See *anchor* or *hypertext link.*

HTML: HyperText Markup Language, the set of commands used to mark up documents with standard elements so they can be displayed and read on the World Wide Web by different browsers on different computers. A subset of SGML (Standard Generalized Markup Language).

HTML Cookie: (Also called the HTML tag.) The tag "set" that makes up a complete HTML markup command. For example, in <B>Attention!</B>, the <B> </B> is the cookie.

HTTP: HyperText Transfer Protocol, the protocol used by Web servers to communicate with Web clients.

Hypertext Links: Also called an anchor. A hypertext link in an HTML document, usually distinguished by underlined or highlighted text that, when selected, takes the user to another file or Web page. The hypertext link is added to the document by using the HTML tag, <A HREF> </A>.

I

IETF: Internet Engineering Task Force, the community of Internet users that determines how the Internet will evolve and operate. Most of its technical operations are conducted in workgroups. Maintains two types of Internet documents, Internet-Drafts and Requests for Comments (RFCs).

Imagemap: A graphic image that has been "mapped" so that every pixel in the image potentially corresponds to a URL. Regions of an imagemap can be drawn which, when the user clicks within the x,y coordinates that define that image (a square, circle, or polygon, for instance), the URL defined by the imagemap author as corresponding to that region appears onscreen.

Index: A service on the Internet, such as Yahoo, that arranges information to help you select what you want to read.

Inline Image: A photo or graphic image that can be displayed in the window of a Web browser along with HTML text (as opposed to an external image, which must be downloaded and viewed with a separate program).

Interlaced Image: An extra step in the information process that enables you to display increasing amounts of information, in quantum leaps, instead of just one line or another. Displays a low-resolution version first, a better version, and then a full-blown version

Internet: An international network of networks, originally started for military purposes, that connects about 40 million higher education, government, military, and commercial users.

IP: Internet Protocol. The set of standards by which information is transmitted on the Internet.

ISDN: Integrated Services Digital Network. A set of standards for transmitting voice, data, and video data simultaneously. A reasonably inexpensive way of getting higher bandwidth through a digital connection.

ISO: International Standards Organization. A group that defines computing and communications standards.

J

Java: Computer language developed by Sun Microsystems that enables the creation of "applets" or "live objects" that execute in response to mouse clicks and produce sound, video, or other effects within Netscape 2.0 or other Web browsers.

JPEG: Joint Photographic Experts Group, a graphic image compression format.

K

Keyword: Word(s) used in a search query.

Knowbot: A type of artificial intelligence software that roams the Web looking for information. You can use a knowbot like KIS (Knowbot Information Service) to find a specific individual's location on the Internet, the name of a Web server, or other information.

L

LAN: Local Area Network. A network usually associated with a single office, building, or organization.

Launch: To start up an application.

Live Object: A clickable element in an HTML document that responds to a user's mouse clicks by producing animation, sound, or other "live" effects within a Web browser window.

Link Location Bar: A text-entry window that contains the URL of the site currently onscreen, or a site, file, or object you want to go to.

M

MacBinary: A standard for storing resources in a Macintosh file's data fork. Also, the name of an application that both decodes and encodes MacBinary files.

MacTCP: Apple Computer software that enables a Macintosh to interact with other computers via TCP/IP.

Memory Cache: A part of a computer's RAM (Random Access Memory, the memory used to run applications) set aside to process/store information.

MIME: Multipurpose Internet Mail Extensions, a standard used for transmitting varying file formats across computing platforms.

Modem: Short for MOdulator/DEModulator. A device that connects a computer to a phone line. It converts the computer's digital signals to analog audio frequencies so they can be transmitted over phone lines.

Mosaic: A graphical information browser for the World Wide Web developed at NCSA. (See *NCSA*.) Its user-friendly interface was instrumental in the Web's popularity.

MPEG: Moving Pictures Experts Group, a movie file format commonly used on the Web.

N

NCSA: National Center for Supercomputing Applications at the University of Illinois at Urbana-Champaign. An interdisciplinary group consisting of scientists, artists, engineers, educators, and others involved in computational science. The place where NCSA Mosaic was born.

Netiquette: A set of rules of behavior on the Internet that cautions against using abusive or offensive language in electronic communications, invading privacy, sending out "chain letters" or unsolicited requests for business, and so on.

Netscape Navigator: A fast, easy-to-use graphical information browser for the World Wide Web that was developed by some of the same people who created Mosaic. Created by Netscape Communications Corporation.

Newbie: A newcomer, someone just getting started on the Internet.

News Server: A machine that collects postings, sorts them, and passes them along to other servers required to use Usenet. Also called a NNTP (Net News Transfer Protocol) server.

NNTP Server: See *News Server.*

NSFNet: National Science Foundation Network, which linked researchers with high-speed supercomputer centers. For a while, this was the "backbone" of the Internet.

P

Parser: A module or routine within a program that reads or "parses" computer code and processes it to make it usable or readable.

PDF: Page Description Format in which documents created with Adobe Acrobat portable document software are presented. Acrobat documents end with the suffix .PDF.

Photoshop: Common parlance for Adobe Photoshop, image editing software that allows a number of sophisticated graphics functions such as retouching and editing of images on personal computers.

ph Server: Served database of email addresses and other personal information about users on a particular network, often maintained by educational institutions.

PICT: A graphics file defined with the Mac's QuickDraw screen description language.

Popup Menu: Generally, this describes any menu that "pops up" on your Macintosh screen; Netscape's main popup menu appears when you click and hold the mouse button over a Web page.

PostScript: A page description/programming language developed by Adobe Systems, Inc. It describes a page in a way that is device-independent so that the quality of the output depends on the resolution of the device on which it is printed.

Private Key: A Web user's personal key, which is never distributed on the Internet, used in public/private key transactions. A key is a very complicated encrypted series of numbers that would take so long to decode that it's essentially unbreakable. Enables a user to read encrypted messages while others cannot.

Progressive JPEG Image: A JPEG image that, like an interlaced GIF image, loads gradually onto your computer and appears onscreen before it is fully loaded, so you can identify an image sooner.

Proportional Fonts: Fonts that vary in width from character to character.

Protocol: A specific method of communication or "conversation" for exchanging information on the Internet. SMTP, FTP, HTTP, and NNTP are all protocols.

Proxy: A software application that is allowed to pass information through a firewall. A firewall is a security system in which one computer, a secure host machine, is the only one in an organization that is actually connected to the Internet. Everyone in the organization must go through the host machine to connect to the Internet, and vice versa.

Public Key: Widely distributed key used in public/private key transactions. A key is a very complicated encrypted series of numbers that would take so long to decode that it's essentially unbreakable. The benefit of a public key is that it is widely available. The fact that a public key is widely available does not lessen security because the public key works only with a private key. (See *Private Key*.)

Q-R

QuickTime: A method developed by Apple Computer for storing movie and audio files in digital format.

QuickTime VR: Hot new format that allows visual representations of scenes wherein you can pan around a full 360 degrees by clicking-and-dragging.

Quote: A button in the Message Composition dialog box that enables you to import the contents of the current page into the text-entry field.

Relevance Feedback: Feature of a Wide Area Information Server (WAIS) that ranks answers judged to be most relevant to your query by putting them highest on a list and scoring them on a scale of 1,000.

RFC: Request for Comments, the agreed-upon designation by which all methods of communicating over the Internet, such as the various versions of HTML, are developed and defined.

Robot: A program such as InfoSeek or Aliweb that searches huge numbers of files automatically when given search criteria (also called a worm).

S

Script Editor: Application that comes with the full AppleScript 1.1 implementation that enables you to build AppleScripts.

Search Engine: A program used by a search service, such as InfoSeek, that takes you through the Internet to find what you want to read. Also called Web "crawlers," "spiders," wanderers," or "worms"; they automatically journey across cyberspace, visiting huge numbers of Web sites and recording titles and some of the contents of individual documents. When you send a search request to a service with such an engine, your request is checked against the index that the engine has already compiled.

Server Push: One way of creating dynamic documents whose contents are refreshed periodically by "pushing" data to your browser.

SGML: Standard Generalized Markup Language, an agreed-upon international standard for specifying and marking up documents. HTML is a subset of SGML.

Shareware: Software created by independent technoids and available for downloading to anyone for a trial time. At the end of that time, users are asked to pay a fee if they decide to keep the software. (See *Freeware.*)

S-HTTP: Secure HyperText Transfer Protocol, a security standard established by EIT/Terisa Systems.

Signature File: A text file appended to the bottom of your email messages and news postings. Commonly called .sig files. Best kept to about four lines.

Silicon Graphics, Inc. (SGI): Silicon Graphics, Inc., a manufacturer of computer hardware and software, including the Indy
workstation. Actively exploring virtual reality applications on the
Web. (See *VRML.*)

.SIT: Filename extension that denotes a file created by one of the
StuffIt software programs, such as StuffIt Expander. Denotes a
"stuffed" or "archived" file.

SLIP: Serial Line Internet Protocol. A way of using TCP/IP over
a serial line, such as a dialup modem. A very common way of
connecting to the Internet from home. Often referred to as a
point-to-point connection. Also lovingly referred to as "slirp."

SMTP: Simple Mail Transfer Protocol. A set of standard proce-
dures for transferring mail.

Spider: See *Search Engine.*

StuffIt Expander: Freeware published by Aladdin Systems that
decodes and decompresses encoded files that have also been
compressed.

Sun: Sun Microsystems, Inc., a company that makes high-
performance workstations and servers using its SPARC architecture. Its Solaris operating system is based on UNIX.

Symmetrical Cryptography: A coding scheme that uses a single
key to encode and decode messages. Some schemes, such as
public key cryptography, require both a public and private key to
decode messages. (See *Public Key* and *Private Key.*)

T

TCP/IP: Transmission Control Protocol/Internet Protocol, a packet-based communication protocol that forms the foundation of the Internet.

Telnet: An application developed at the University of Illinois that acts as a sort of intermediary application to other programs running on remote computers on the Internet.

TIFF: Tagged Image File Format, a format for storing computerized image files.

Title Bar: Appears at the top of the screen; gives you the title of the document currently displayed.

Transparent GIF: A GIF image that appears to float directly atop a Web page without its own background or border. A specific number in the GIF color palette (#89) is assigned to be the same color as the background of the page, giving the image a transparent appearance.

U-W

UNIX: A multiuser/multitasking operating system developed by AT&T and written in the C programming language (also developed by AT&T). Its TCP/IP protocols are integral to the Internet.

URL: Uniform Resource Locator. A standard address for a file or location on the Internet. URLs always begin with an Internet protocol (FTP, Gopher, HTTP), an Internet host name, folders, and the destination file or object.

Usenet Newsgroups: A global computer network run by the community of Internet users that can be accessed either from within or outside the Internet. (Usenet is short for User's Network.) A tremendously popular means of sharing information over the Internet. Usenet is older and more extensive than the Web.

VRML: Virtual Reality Modeling Language (VRML; sometimes pronounced "vur-mole"). It has been proposed as a standard way of describing virtual reality experiences accessed via the Internet and integrated with the hypertextual power of the Web.

WAIS: Wide Area Information Server. WAIS was developed as a way of allowing big businesses to search for electronic information quickly and easily from a large number of sources by using English-language queries.

WAN: Wide Area Network. A communications system that spans great distances, as opposed to a LAN.

Web Crawler: See *Search Engine.*

Web Project: A term used to describe a collection of Web pages that are in development. Web projects are independent of the Web servers that serve them.

Web Server: A computer set up to exchange information with another computer over the Internet using one or more standard protocols, such as HTTP, FTP, Gopher, and so on.

Web Site: A collection of Web pages residing on a Web server. Web sites are usually synonymous with a URL. One server can host several Web sites by providing URLs that define a path to the Web site. Some types of computers can support multiple unique URLs on a single server.

Webmaster: Someone who both creates Web pages and manages a Web server.

Webpublisher: A person who creates Web pages.

What's Cool: A page on Netscape's Web site that lists "cool" sites you might want to visit.

What's New: A page on Netscape's Web site that lists pages that have recently come online.

World Wide Web (Web): A subset of the Internet that enables hypertextual navigation and multimedia presentation of information globally.

Worm: See *Search Engine.*

X-Z

.ZIP: Filename extension for a file created by PKZip, the standard compression software used in the world of DOS and Windows.

Index

A

B

G

Q-R

Y–Z

Create Awesome Macintosh Web Sites!

If you currently use or want to use the power and ease of the Macintosh to create awesome Web sites, you should attend Mactivity/Web-San Francisco. Whether you are an advanced, intermediate, or beginning Webmaster, Mactivity/Web has sessions tailored to your needs.

Attend one of these educational events and learn the practical skills you need to create exciting, informative, Mac-based Web sites that incorporate CGIs and Java applets, interact with your current computer databases, and keep people returning to your site again and again.

If you want a winning Web site, attend Mactivity/Web.

Wicked smart people. Wicked cool products.

Conferences held at several locations around the country.

At Mactivity/Web, you'll:

- See the latest Macintosh Web publishing technology: JAVA, VRML, SSL, Netscape 2.0
- Try out your newly-learned skills in our hands-on labs

- Extend the power of your Web site without programming
- Explore new tools and products
- Create clickable imagemaps for use on your Macintosh Web site
- Integrate your Macintosh Web site with databases
- Learn how to do business on the Web legally and profitably
  … and much more!

Call **1-800-798-2928** for a brochure or browse www.mactivity.com.

We'll see you at "The Ultimate World Wide Web Developers Conference© !"

For more info call **1-800-798-2928** or visit www.mactivity.com.

"This is the most informative, most innovative conference about the World Wide Web. You'll find everything you need to know to build a better Web site."

Nathan Shedroff,
Creative Director,
vivid studios, award-winning
Web design firm

design
solutions
from hayden books

REGISTRATION CARD

Insert Book Title Here

Hayden Books

Name _____ Title _____

Company_____Type of business _____

Address _____

City/State/ZIP _____

Have you used these types of books before? ☐ yes ☐ no

If yes, which ones? _____

_____

How many computer books do you purchase each year? ☐ 1–5 ☐ 6 or more

How did you learn about this book?_____

    ☐ recommended by a friend   ☐ received ad in mail

    ☐ recommended by store personnel   ☐ read book review

    ☐ saw in catalog   ☐ saw on bookshelf

Where did you purchase this book? _____

Which applications do you currently use? _____

Which computer magazines do you subscribe to? _____

What trade shows do you attend? _____

Please number the top three factors which most influenced your decision for this book purchase.

    ☐ cover   ☐ price

    ☐ approach to content   ☐ author's reputation

    ☐ logo   ☐ publisher's reputation

    ☐ layout/design   ☐ other _____

Would you like to be placed on our preferred mailing list? ☐ yes ☐ no e-mail address _____

☐ **I would like to see my name in print!** You may use my name and quote me in future Hayden products and promotions. My daytime phone number is: _____

Comments _____

_____

_____

Hayden Books   Attn: Product Marketing ◆ 201 West 103rd Street ◆ Indianapolis, Indiana 46290 USA

Fax to **317-581-3576**   Visit out Web Page **http://WWW.MCP.com/hayden/**

Fold Here

- -

BUSINESS REPLY MAIL
FIRST-CLASS MAIL PERMIT NO. 9918 INDIANAPOLIS IN

POSTAGE WILL BE PAID BY THE ADDRESSEE

HAYDEN BOOKS
Attn: Product Marketing
201 W 103RD ST
INDIANAPOLIS IN 46290-9058

EXHIBIT C

ADOBE SYSTEMS INCORPORATED
MINIMUM TERMS OF END USER AGREEMENTS

1 Licensor grants Licensee a non-exclusive sublicense to use the Adobe software ("Software") and the related written materials ("Documentation") provided by Adobe Systems Incorporated ("Adobe") to Licensor as set forth below. Licensee may install and use the Software on one computer.

2 The Software is owned by Adobe and its suppliers and its structure, organization, and code are the valuable trade secrets of Adobe and its suppliers. Licensee agrees not to modify, adapt, translate, reverse engineer, decompile, disassemble or otherwise attempt to discover the source code of the Software. Licensee agrees not to attempt to increase the functionality of the Software in any manner. Licensee agrees that any permitted copies of the Software shall contain the same copyright and other proprietary notices which appear on and in the Software.

3 Except as stated above, this Agreement does not grant Licensee any right (whether by license, ownership or otherwise) in or to intellectual property with respect to the Software.

4 Licensee will not export or re-export the Software Programs without the appropriate United States or foreign government licenses.

5 Trademarks, if used by Licensee shall be used in accordance with accepted trademark practice, including identification of the trademark owner's name. Trademarks can only be used to identify printed output produced by the Software. The use of any trademark as herein authorized does not give Licensee rights of ownership in that trademark.

6 LICENSEE ACKNOWLEDGES THAT THE SOFTWARE IS A "TRY-OUT" VERSION OF AN ADOBE PRODUCT, CON- TAINING LIMITED FUNCTIONALITY. ADOBE IS LICENSING THE SOFTWARE ON AN "AS-IS" BASIS, AND ADOBE AND ITS SUPPLIERS MAKE NO WARRANTIES EXPRESSED OR IMPLIED, INCLUDING, WITHOUT LIMITATION, AS TO NON-INFRINGEMENT OF THIRD PARTY RIGHTS, MERCHANTABILITY, OR FITNESS FOR ANY PARTICULAR PURPOSE. IN NO EVENT WILL ADOBE OR ITS SUPPLIERS BE LIABLE TO LICENSEE FOR ANY CONSEQUENTIAL, INCIDENTAL OR SPECIAL DAMAGES, INCLUDING ANY LOST PROFITS OR LOST SAVINGS, EVEN IF REPRESENTA- TIVES OF SUCH PARTIES HAVE BEEN ADVISED OF THE POSSIBILITY OF SUCH DAMAGES, OR FOR ANY CLAIM BY ANY THIRD PARTY.

IF A SHRINKWRAP LICENSEE IS USED [Some states or jurisdictions do not allow the exclusion or limitation of inciden- tal, consequential or special damages, so the above limitation or exclusion may not apply to Licensee. Also some states or jurisdictions do not allow the exclusion of implied warranties or limitation on how long an implied warranty may last, so the above limitations may not apply to Licensee. To the extent permissible, any implied warranties are limited to ninety (90) days. This warranty gives Licensee specific legal rights. Licensee may have other rights which vary from state to state or jurisdiction to jurisdiction.]

7 Notice to Government End Users: If this product is acquired under the terms of a: <u>GSA contract:</u> Use, reproduction or disclosure is subject to the restrictions set forth in the applicable ADP Schedule contract. <u>DoD contract</u>: Use, duplication or disclosure by the Government is subject to restrictions as set forth in subparagraph (c) (1) (ii) of 252.227-7013. <u>Civilian agency contract</u>: Use, reproduction or disclosure is subject to 52.227-19 (a) through (d) and restrictions set forth in the accompanying end user agreement. Unpublished-rights reserved under the copyright laws of the United States.

CD Contents

The Adobe® PageMill™ demo application.

A self-guided PageMill™ tutorial.

Information on obtaining a full version of PageMill™.

PageMill™ templates.

Sample images.

Exercise files.

An application program that helps you create tables on your Web pages.

To Install your demo copy of Adobe® PageMill™:

Insert the PageMill Handbook CD into your CD-ROM drive.

Double-click on the PageMill Handbook™ CD icon and open the PageMill Evaluation Package folder.

Double-click on the Install PageMill™ icon.

Follow the onscreen instructions to install your demo copy of PageMill™.

The folder created on your hard drive contains the demo application and the EarthandWareTutorial.